VOLUME 2

WAITING IN THE
PIT

TESTIMONIES OF TESTS, TEARS, TRIALS AND TRIUMPHS

VISIONARY AUTHOR
HILETTE A. VIRGO

©2023 Hilette Virgo. All rights reserved.

All rights reserved. No portion of this book may be reproduced, stored in a retrieval system, or transmitted in any form or by any means – electronic, mechanical, photocopy, recording, scanning, or other – except for a brief quotation in critical reviews or articles, without the prior written permission of the publisher or author.

Published by:

Cover designed by Serena Rowe

Unless otherwise stated, all Scriptures are taken from the KING JAMES VERSION (KJV): KING JAMES VERSION, public domain.

Dedication

This book is dedicated to those who have waited, those in the throes of waiting, and those who have yet to wait on the Lord.

You shall mount up with Eagle's wings. (Isaiah 40:31)

Introduction

I knew I had heard correctly. Everything else aligned and made sense. I got the download, acted promptly, and like the most beautiful tapestry, the weft threads were intricately woven, creating a mind-blowing masterpiece. We celebrated, cried, laughed, beamed, and commended each other. One big happy family gathered in the pit of God's hands, glorifying Him for the work He had inspired, collaborated with, and ushered successfully through the beaming tunnel-end of authorship.

The breakthrough testimonies flowed as we gleefully rode the currents, cheerfully wading in hilarity and delight. I paused as I remembered what the Holy Spirit revealed that fateful day I embarked on the vessel of fasting and prayer. I felt honored that He chose me to captain and berth this ship, but something was missing. We had a pact, didn't we? Wasn't I supposed to cash out on a breakthrough as well? I had specifics. I went into fasting and prayer, purposely asking for three things, and the agreement was that I would receive my heart's desire at the book's release—or so I thought.

I did my part and believed with all my heart that a breakthrough was sent through divine mail with my name artfully inscribed and

Introduction

would land on my doorsteps expressly. I watched daily, waiting for it to arrive. To see others testifying about what God had done for them on account of taking this unforeseen path of the pen left a bitter-bland taste in my mouth.

Okay, I may need to wait a few more months. After all, isn't waiting the theme of my life? Maybe my cake required more time after coming from the oven before I could partake. Of course, given my experience with watching my mother bake and decorate cakes for years, I knew there was a process of allowing the cake to cool, mixing the icing, bagging, piping, rolling, and intricately designing the cake. I had to wait a little longer and cool down from all the excitement, get a little mixed here and there, and have the Holy Spirit bag, pipe, and roll me over to prepare for the display table. I was ready! I had released the burden of shame and all the nuances associated with the story I shared in my chapter, which the writing process usually facilitates. I was sure I was no longer in the dug-out, self-pity pit I had frightfully huddled in at the foot of the cross or in the pit of condemnation I was thrust in. I was now safely nestled in the hollow of God's hand as a fruit pit, beautifully broken to bear fruit.

Snuggled in a place of safety, I suppose I can wait a little longer.

A few months in, I was restless. If I am to be a bearer of truth, I was downright disappointed, angry, and bitter with God. *How much longer? Why? Is this waiting season going to end anytime soon? Do you even love me, God? Why must I languish in this place of singleness and unmet expectations? Where are you? Was I mistaken?* (Tears of recollection).

Waiting In the Pit

I had composed grandiose plans to host a series of book launches in several churches in Georgia, USA, where I resided. I had already gotten confirmation from the pastor of the church I visited frequently and from Pastor Patrick Carter, one of the co-authors who shepherded a church in Atlanta to host launches. However, I was no longer excited about the project. I felt rejected and dejected. Why bother?

A date was already established for the first launch, where I was rostered to speak. Banners, playing the book trailer, and a book signing at the end of the Sabbath were on the running order. It was supposed to be a celebration, reflection, and inspiration day. My event planning expertise had gone into full thrust when the idea first hatched, but now, I was deflated. I had no interest, energy, or drive to tell people it was worth waiting on the Lord. How could I when I felt scammed? Many of the other authors got their testimonies. They were riding the tides of social media, securing radio and podcast interviews, writing, and publishing their memoir books that I had encouraged them to write, and just singing high praises. Yet, the visionary had nothing personal to speak of, even though I was convinced that the Holy Spirit had told me a breakthrough was guaranteed.

Three Sabbaths after the event, my pastor, Shaun Brooks, approached me to confirm the date. I asked if we could reschedule for a few months away, possibly in the new year. The man of God looked at me and told me not to cancel or postpone but to pray about it.

I refused to pray; I had already decided that I didn't want to do it. While sitting in church the following week during the divine hour

Introduction

of worship, I received another download. God gave me a message I had no interest in presenting. *How much more do you require of me, Lord? And why should I preach a sermon that would implicate me?*

The Lord said. "You say you are waiting on me, but I have been waiting on you." In keeping with my preaching style, he downloaded the acronym WAITING. As I resisted the download, He gently poured liter by liter of the water of life into my empty jar over the following weeks up until the morning of delivery. There was no escape; I had to present. My name was etched in the bulletin, the pastor announced it on a flyer on his social media page, friends all over the world committed to watching the live stream, Carlene, my new friend, had planned to drive two hours, and my Nigerian bestie, Happy, and her family, had already planned to surprise me at church that day. The Holy Spirit wouldn't let me disappoint my friends or the hearts He had already prepared, plowed, and positioned for the message. No ships were heading to Tarshish, and I was the Ninevite who needed the message.

There were no banners, trailers, book copies, or anything commercially related. That day, I showed up stripped of expectations, subdued by His ministering, and spiritually straddled. I cautioned the congregation that I came to preach on myself. I told them to take whatever the message held for them and leave the rest.

As my eight-year-old daughter would say, I "snitched" on myself. The message went like this:

God was waiting on me to:

Wake up: from my slumber. Like Peter, James, and John, who went to pray with Jesus and fell asleep (Matthew 26:36-46), and the five foolish virgins (Matthew 25:1-13), I was sleeping in my spiritual life. I had a form of godliness but denied the power thereof (2 Timothy 3:5). I did not engage the Holy Spirit as I should, and my lamp had run out of oil. The Savior was expecting me to tarry with Him as He petitioned for the souls of men, and I fell asleep on Him.

Worship Him: in Spirit and truth. I was giving God what I thought or felt I should give. The song: *"What if God is unhappy with our praise"* came to mind. I was not worshipping Him on His terms but mine. I gave Him what I felt, expecting Him to accept any scrap. I forgot that God had His standards, and as His follower, I had a responsibility to abide by them accordingly. I could not worship Him how and when I felt, but as the Word required.

Act Right: For years, I was busy throwing tantrums, whining, and pining. God was waiting for me to develop the right attitude to give me my heart's desire. In my state, I was in no position to receive my breakthrough.

Avail myself/ be accountable: Even though I was obedient in getting the book done, much more was required. Too often, I didn't avail myself to be used in His service. I was also not taking responsibility and accountability for my shortcomings. It was easy to blame the devil and others when things went awry. He was waiting on me to take stock and inventory of my spiritual life and repent.

Introduction

Incline my ear: God was waiting on me to shut up and listen. Every week I sang the song, *"Hear my prayers, Oh Lord!"* asking God to incline His ear to me. But how often did I listen to Him speaking? I was good at requesting and beseeching the Lord, but I had challenges hearing Him speak because I had a spiritual hearing impairment and spent too much time in the noise.

Inspire others: I felt for years that I had this one in the bag. Wasn't that what I specialized in? I was a Christian life coach and motivational speaker. The question is, was I drawing others to myself or God? Was my inspiration God-led and God-centered? Or was I creating followers and fans for myself?

Testify: I always felt I was big on testimonies. I loved giving praise reports and testifying. However, what was the motive? Was I selective with my testimonies, sharing only those that would put me in a favorable light? Was God getting all the glory?

Need Him: For so long, I was leaning on my understanding and treating God as an ATM, showing up when I needed a favor or material things or when I hit rock bottom. God was waiting on me to need Him as much as I needed sleep, oxygen, food, water, and a bath. He wanted me to see Him as my place of rest, the air I breathe, the Bread of Life, Living Water, and the One who cleanses and purifies me of my sins.

Nestle in His presence: God awaited me to see Him as my refuge. In the same manner that I found my mother's lap as a place of safety and comfort when I was a child, God was waiting on me to nestle in His lap and bask in His sweet presence.

Be Grateful: He was also waiting on me to develop a heart, spirit, and attitude of gratitude. I was a chronic complainer, and in the seizure spells of my complaints, I could not see the table He had prepared before me. I was lost in my problems that I did not see the promotion He had given me; buried under my challenges, I did not see the chances He gave me to elevate and excel.

And finally...

Give myself completely to Him: God was waiting for me to surrender fully.

Every good deal or gift comes with conditions, and there is no exception with God. He loves us unconditionally, but His promises are conditional. He often withholds things from us when we are not mature enough to handle them. Premature breakthroughs can be spiritually fatal. In His wisdom, God knows that if He gives us something that we are not prepared and ready for, we may not appreciate it, or it may harm us and others. Hence, God has me waiting in my pit for my soul's salvation. Still!

I sat down with Him, and He revealed that this project was not about me. It was far more significant! It suddenly dawned on me that I had gotten a more extraordinary breakthrough than I had imagined—a spiritual one. Like Jabez, He enlarged my territory, but not materially. He has drafted me as a codirector to usher others into the beautiful author orchestra.

Serving and engaging twenty other souls, most of whom have never seen themselves as capable of authorship, He has sharpened my literary, leadership, and communication skills. The lights came off me, and I was forced to see how honorable a role I was given

Introduction

to partner behind the scenes with the Holy Spirit in coaching, organizing, editing, assembling the chapters, and navigating all the processes for its successful release.

Additionally, the Holy Spirit told me to revisit the contractual terms. From day one, I knew the anthology was a three-part series. However, I thought my breakthrough was at the end of volume one. God showed me I needed more work and refining. Therefore, the breakthrough I craved was at the end of the third volume. Also, part of my process was organizing and managing the publishing of the volumes.

I am no longer as obsessed with claiming a breakthrough, but I am in awe of what God is doing for, with, and through His children as He furnishes and approves them for authorship, ministry, and service. He stands before them as they wait or are waiting, using the melodies of their stories to create a symphony to bless and beautify the souls of others.

Sitting stunningly in the orchestra pit are the musicians God handpicked to liven and bless your soul. I now present to you, *Waiting in the Pit II*.

Enjoy the mellow notes of the trombone; the warm tones of the violin; the buzzing of the brass; the deep rich vibrations of the cello; the low-pitched notes of the tuba, double bass, and bassoon; the loud rhythms of the trumpet; the whistling sounds of the oboe; the fluid notes of the clarinet, the high pitched sounds, and rhythm of the flute and piccolo; the sweet harmonies of the timpani; the beautiful sounds of the harp; the soft-loud notes of the piano; the brazen tinge of the saxophone, and the clashing of the cymbals.

Jesus Christ, the Master Director, has assembled this symphony orchestra of beautiful souls whose tests, tears, trials, and triumphs have created a magical harmony of notes to woo, bless and pull on the strings of your heart. May the melodies draw you closer to Christ and leave you inspired and impressed to surrender to the workings of the Holy Spirit.

> *"The Lord is good to those who wait for him, to the soul who seeks him."* **Lamentations 3:25**

Acknowledgement

Special thanks to the twenty-one instrumentalists who said yes to playing in this literary symphony orchestra. Thank you for allowing the Holy Spirit to use you to bear your souls and share some of your most vulnerable stories. For many, tapping on the skin of their soul to release the melody was painful. Several went breathless, queuing the chords and blowing out shame, pain, and frustration, and others had challenges tuning their heartstrings.

It was a beautiful experience watching you rehearse, clean, and polish your stories' lines as you waited in the pit for the Light to illuminate you. You trusted the Director and co-director and played excellently.

Thanks to Dr. Joan Rickets and Felonie Johnson for putting the finishing touches on the composition. We appreciate you.

Special thanks to our stage and technical managers, Serena Rowe and Colbert Simpson. Thanks for the beautiful cover designs, trailers, and mockups accompanying this production.

The Lord has done it once more, and we are grateful. Blessed be His name.

Table of Contents

Introduction 4

Acknowledgement 13

Chapter 1: The Snake Pit 17

Meet Sharon Correia 28

Chapter 2: Pit of Self-Sabotage 29

Meet Carlene Francis 44

Chapter 3: Saved In the Pit 45

Meet Tashina Morrison 55

Chapter 4: The Bi-sexual Woman at the Well 56

Meet Shasta Green 67

Chapter 5: Descending Deeper in the Pit 68

Meet Serena Rowe 78

Chapter 6: Pit of Grace 79

Table of Contents

Meet Joy Pilgrim-Briggs 89

Chapter 7: Stacked Coal Pit 90

Meet Angelic Lezama-Clement 104

Chapter 8: Purpose In My Pit 105

Meet Shauna-Kaye Brown 115

Chapter 9: Something Better after Waiting 116

Meet Yanet Ruth Guarachi 127

Chapter 10: Pit of Shame and Unforgiveness 128

Meet Carlene Peters 139

Chapter 11: Pit of Alienation 140

Meet Miguel Lowe 148

Chapter 12: My Pit Stop 149

Meet Evett James 159

Chapter 13: The Bitter Experiences in my Marital Pit ... 160

Chapter 13.5: The Ticket out of my Pit 172

Meet Stephanie Minto-Hinds 183

Chapter 14: Restored in the Pit 184

Meet Nadian "Lady Theresa" Reid 197

Chapter 15: Pit Hopping 198

Meet Daphine Douglas 208

Chapter 16: Rescued from the Pit of Abuse 209

Meet Deneve Sweeney 216

Chapter 17: The Beauty of the Morning 217

Meet Maria Urassa 227

Chapter 18: Will I Ever See the Light of Day? 228

Meet Robert Vassell 238

Chapter 19: The Pit of Pain and Suffering 239

Meet Joleen Meharris-Simpson 250

Chapter 20: Why live when you want to die? 251

Meet Candice Andrews 262

Chapter 21: Waiting Well 263

Meet Patricia Salmon 274

Meet the Visionary 276

CHAPTER 1

The Snake Pit

*"The name of the LORD is a strong tower: the righteous runneth into it and is safe." **(Proverbs 18:10)***

This chapter delves into experiences surrounding the occult and the supernatural. Our God is a mighty God who has all power over all demons and evil powers. Be covered in His shadow therefore as you read, remembering **Ephesians 6:12.**

This is an experience I had at a teachers' training college in Guyana, South America. I liken our experience to being caught amid a den of pit vipers equipped with the sensory heat receptors that allow them to sense prey in the dark.

Fifteen terrified young trainee teachers huddled together in a tiny dorm room designed for two. The fear was palpable. Through the wooden slats of the painted green panel doors, we could see numerous feet, intent on mischief, approaching. They came scuttling down the corridor towards us.

Waiting In the Pit

Something from another realm, dark and sinister, had been unleashed on campus. Some of our batch mates had been transformed into demented howling creatures with baleful red eyes and foam-flecked mouths. They almost seemed as though they were slithering. Closer and closer, they came, tightening the invisible noose around our sense of safety. The only welcomed movement in that room was to cower even lower behind the desks and twin cots. Even the crawl spaces under the two closets were occupied. We linked hands even as we lay. Some were silent as the rest of us prayed earnestly into the silence.

It had all begun a week prior to the Christmas break of that year. The young men from the adjacent male dormitory had decided to liven up the atmosphere by singing Christmas carols and banging away on some makeshift drums. One of the boys seemed particularly adept at beating his drum. He passionately tapped a steady, heady, pulsating rhythm. The girls gathered in the lounge, listening intently to the entertainment.

One girl began to sway in a strange trance-like way, much like a cobra, moving to the music of a snake charmer. Encouraged, the young man beat his drum faster, louder. The girl began to whirl and contort her body in impossible positions. Her eyes had taken on a strange gleam. She seemed transported to another realm. The wild dance movements became frantic. Our collective jaws dropped in astonished fear.

In a moment, she was joined by another, then another. Soon, there was a mass of bodies writhing and wriggling on the floor in the most frightening, serpentine way. The hairs on our skin bristled. The guys, their eyes wide with fright, dropped all their

The Snake Pit

paraphernalia and bolted from the building. Then, the horrid frenzy began in earnest.

The girls were convulsing and contorting. There was now a small army of them. The evil thing spread its tentacles wide, sucking them deeper into the quagmire. The music was over, but they couldn't stop themselves. Instead of dancing, their movements became even more frenzied and chaotic. Pandemonium was the order of the day. Piercing screams rent the air. One of those girls had accomplished the impossible feat of standing on her head and whirling her body in a curious undulating movement. The others followed her cue. Their eyes took on an unnatural glare, much like the eyes of wild predatory animals. They whirled in unison. It seemed like some sort of macabre dance. Their torsos undulated, their eyes wild and gleaming. An image of huge hissing pit vipers rushed unbidden into my mind.

They began tearing furiously at their hair and clothing. Fear was a live thing. We all made a mad dash from the immediate area. Pandemonium reigned as the word spread. All the occupants of the dorms, both male and female students, fled in terror. A more disheveled and distressed bunch, you'd be hard-pressed to find. People could be heard screaming for their parents or spouses, anyone with whom they shared a close relationship. I was a student from the hinterland region of Guyana, so all my immediate family were hundreds of miles away.

I could only call on God!

From childhood, I was taught to call on the mighty name of Jesus when facing adversity. There are countless episodes in my life where I am convinced that only the power of Almighty God saved me. Once, I had come face to face with a bushmaster snake, the largest pit viper in the world and the second-largest venomous snake after the king cobra. That particular snake is a master of camouflage. The snake had neatly ensconced itself in a pile of firewood that we used for cooking. The diamond-shaped patterns on its back blended so well with the colors of the wood that the venomous reptile was barely detectable. I was about to step closer to the pile when I saw horrid, beady eyes staring coldly into mine. I will never forget the malignancy of that gaze. Because it was snugly fitted between the firewood, I was able to move quickly out of harm's way.

I was certain God had sent an angel to protect me that day. As I looked at the transformation of those girls in the dorms, I remembered that bushmaster and its baleful evil eyes. By this time, the feral group of feverishly dancing girls had more than tripled. Their present mannerisms made them seem as though they were hunting prey. They began to move methodically, sweeping through the corridors of both dormitories. The students moved like a school of herrings, with killer sharks closing in on them. They spilled every which way into the grounds of the college.

When Jesus had healed the demon-possessed man from among the tombs, Jesus asked the demon's name, and the demon answered. The name was "Legion" because there were many of them. They had maddened the herd of swine into which they were cast.

The Snake Pit

I saw a similar scenario unfolding. I began mumbling prayers as the human tide of students swept me in the direction of the campus grounds.

Twilight had already set in, pinning millions of stars in place. They twinkled like diamonds against the dark purple blanket of the night sky. As we spilled into the lush green grass, the full moon bathed the area with silvern light. This would have usually appeared ethereal in its beauty. This time, the moonlight seemed chillingly eerie. The nearby bushes cast long dark shadows, which lent to the illusion of evil, creeping, crawling, slithering things coming to get us. I shivered in apprehension, still mumbling my prayers through numb lips.

Guyana is a country that is situated smack into the heart of the Amazon Rainforest. There are myriad insects and strange nocturnal and diurnal animals that reside there. The crickets, frogs, owls, toads, etc., kept up a steady cacophony of eerie sounds. When coupled with the shadows and the shrieking, maniacal girls, these sounds sent fear and panic soaring throughout the compound. A pall of impending doom descended upon us all.

As a child, if you have been brought up in a God-fearing family, your faith is implicit. As you get older, the pressures of life can sometimes cause you to question that faith. I had sometimes felt as though God was very, very far away. I can truly testify that my faith in God was restored a hundred-fold that night. I silently prayed in earnest, though my eyes were wide open. I petitioned the Creator of the Universe to save us from the evil surrounding us.

Waiting In the Pit

The college campus was some twenty miles from the capital city of Georgetown, Guyana—sprawling buildings with spacious green lawns interspersed with giant almond trees. A few small villages surrounded the college. Beyond those villages, there were many acres of rice fields. About two hundred yards away from the rice fields roared the mighty Atlantic Ocean; huge murky waves crashed against the barriers of the "sea walls."

Guyana does not have the clear blue water of other Caribbean nations. This is due to the mighty flow of the enormous rivers, namely the Amazon, Orinoco, and Essequibo, pushing silt into the ocean. The sea walls, an engineering feat of great magnitude, were built by the Dutch in the 1500s, during the colonial era. The Dutch had reclaimed land from the sea; that's why the city of Georgetown lies approximately six feet below sea level and is surrounded by the massive infrastructure we call sea walls.

At that time of the evening, public transportation was almost non-existent. Beyond the boundaries of the campus were a few tiny villages, which were without adequate street lighting. These villages were the favorite haunts of many unsavory characters. Just walking there at night was fraught with danger. We were literally caught between the Devil and the deep brown sea. Everyone huddled together, trying to draw strength from each other. We looked towards the entrance to the dorms. The feral bunch had taken up positions in front of the entrance of the girls' dormitory. Wildly blazing eyes dared anyone to try and escape.

Someone ran for the warden, who came charging out of his quarters like a maddened bull. The warden was a stockily built man who prided himself on his well-honed physique. He seemed

The Snake Pit

the epitome of "fit and fearless." He called the first girl by name. She raised bloodshot eyes to his and, with a snarl, pounced and grabbed him by his shirt. His shirt was reduced to ribbons in seconds, and blood oozed from long scratches on his arms and upper torso. That strongly muscled man fought like a maniac against that young woman, who seemed charged with supernatural strength. She tried her utmost to claw his eyes out. He wrestled her to the ground, fighting like a prize fighter. He gradually overpowered her and ran for his life, much like our students.

A mass of growling, spitting human beings emerged from the corners of the buildings. We heard the awful sound of breaking glass. Unseen forces shattered the windows of some of the rooms. In certain villages of the country, spiritual rituals involving the beating of drums to summon ancestral spirits are still observed. Some of the frenzied bunch hailed from such villages.

It was utter chaos. People ran helter-skelter all over the campus. The rabid maniacal girls chased after all and sundry. They tore the clothing, clawed at the eyes, and bit anyone who had the misfortune to get caught by them. They displayed feats of supernatural strength, hurling massive objects around. Horrors of horrors, now some were seen grabbing the shards of glass from the broken windows. Their hands bled as they cut themselves. The sight of blood seemed to whip them into an even greater frenzy. Blood-curdling shrieks rent the night.

We watched in horror as the wailing, snarling girls formed a horseshoe formation on the concrete pathways connecting the male and female dorms. Suddenly! One of those girls took the lead. She barked at the others in a high-pitched, shrill voice. Her utterances couldn't be deciphered by any of us regular students. I suspect that no normal person could comprehend either. Unbelievably, the others stayed still, listening intently, their wild eyes fixed on her. Their leader chattered incessantly. We could see heads bobbing in assent. To us, it seemed as though they were planning some deadly mode of attack, and she was giving the orders.

This gathering of the unlovely gave us a brief respite. As they congregated, everyone took the opportunity to beat a hasty retreat for their rooms via the back entrance of the dorms. Students from Georgetown and other outlying areas stealthily emerged from their rooms, grabbed whatever belongings they could, and beat a hasty exit on foot via the rice fields and back roads. Those of us who hailed from other regions were not so fortunate. We had no family or relatives in the city or its environs. We had to stay put. What a night to remember!

My roommate and I ran for our room. A short while later, several of our batchmates banged on the door of our tiny room. We gingerly opened the door and let them in. "Can we all pray together?" they pleaded. In the face of imminent danger, people of all faiths united. We linked hands and prayed as never before. We called on our Shepherd, Jesus Christ, to rescue us, His sheep. As we were deep into praying, we heard a chilling sound. A rasping voice pierced the air, screeching the name of one of the girls in the room with us. Maniacal laughter ricocheted all around as the voice intoned her name. Everyone's hair stood on end. We shivered with fright, wondering what ghastly event they were planning.

They came, skulking up the corridors, with the purposeful intent of securing their quarry. We placed her in the middle of our group and summoned the forces of Heaven, praying as never before. As they approached, I felt as though unseen arms were enfolding us. I was sure God had sent an army of angels to protect us. Psalms 34:7, "The Angel of the LORD encampeth round about them that fear him, and delivereth them."

The possessed girls headed straight for our room. Slowly, methodically, they advanced. Their leader's gaze locked on mine. A shiver ran down my spine. Like the venomous pit viper, her eyes were the coldest I'd ever gazed upon. I looked into them; they were chillingly devoid of any expression. I immediately recognized what was before me. She was undoubtedly under the control of the one known as the ancient serpent. An icy cold finger of fear caressed my spine, but even at that moment, I knew that the unseen mighty angels of God's army were protecting us. Of that, I was confident.

As our prayers filled the room, the feral gazes became confused. A warm, secure feeling entered my body. A look of utter fear overcame those unspeakable countenances. We prayed even more fervently. They stopped, averted their gazes, and backed away from the door. God had surely opened their eyes to behold the angels that were guarding us. They slunk away, rushing headlong down the flight of stairs to the courtyard below. We didn't move until we were certain they were no longer around. We did not sleep a wink that entire night.

The first pink blush of dawn arrived, and with it came a renewal of spirits. We cautiously exited the room. Everyone seemed very quiet. Even the boisterous kitchen staff spoke in hushed tones. In the corner of the auditorium, huddled the grisly bunch. Everyone backed away from them suspiciously, but they remained very still.

The warden approached; a collection of blank stares fixed on him. He called them by their names. They answered as though they were in a trance. Not one of them remembered anything that had transpired during the night. They seemed lost and confused. Their eyes, though calmer, still held a vestige of wildness. The warden and resident tutors herded them to their respective rooms. Their family members were contacted, and they were escorted off campus that very day.

Everyone else had also made arrangements to leave the compound. We later learned that someone from the ground staff at the college had passed away a few days before. The body had been taken to the college grounds, and one of those gruesome, spiritual rituals was performed. Maybe that had opened a gateway to the spirit realm.

The college was immediately closed for the semester, although it was one week shy of the closing date. Except for a skeleton staff, the campus was left vacant.

It was truly one of the most harrowing experiences of my life. We shivered with apprehension at what we thought was the inevitable outcome. Everyone was drenched in cold sweat. At one point, it got so bad that some girls grimaced in pain because of the knots in their stomachs. Some were physically ill after that experience. We followed the Bible's admonition to watch and pray, quite literally. I will unreservedly say that it was truly a miracle that no one got trampled, beaten, or stabbed to death that night. I have never again witnessed anything close to this, for which I am grateful.

We returned with some trepidation for the new semester. All was well! Great news! The first girl who came under the serpentine spirit had given her life to Jesus. The change in her was remarkable. She was resolute in her devotion to God and became a stalwart in God's army of devout Christians. She's now firmly grounded in faith.

Sometimes, in this life journey, we face situations in which we know that there's only one source of help—the kind of help which only comes from our Creator. Whether we raise our eyes heavenward, whisper under our breaths or cry aloud; we must trust that God is always in control. I knew only divine intervention could get us out of this pit of fear and impending doom.

I have concluded that if fear is contagious, love will be even more so, as the two emotions are more powerful. As we waited that fateful night in the snake pit of doom, love extended its loving heel and crushed the serpent's head.

John 4:11 says, "There's no fear in love, but perfect love casts out fear."

God is Love, the perfect antidote to fear.

Meet Sharon Correia

Sharon Correia is a former teacher who hails from the country of Guyana, South America. She presently works as a senior hairstylist in a prestigious salon in the Cayman Islands.

She writes stories in standard English as well as Guyana Creole. Some of her stories have been featured on Pablo's Kreolese Corner, based in Atlanta. She writes articles for a Guyanese group, "Guyana A Story of Pictures, Old, and New," which comprises 130,000 + members. Here's a sample of the many reviews she has received:

"I am a writer, but this ode to a mother's love is so super-excellent that I am moved to the depths of my heart. I cannot imagine the depths of your nightmarish lifetime pain." Parvati Edwards.

She is a devout Christian who serves as assistant children's ministry leader of Bodden Town SDA, Grand Cayman.

She can be contacted at sharonb112@yahoo.com

CHAPTER 2

Pit of Self-Sabotage

"For thy Maker is thine husband; the Lord of hosts is his name; and thy Redeemer the Holy One of Israel; The God of the whole earth shall he be called." **(Isaiah 54:5)**

"Are you okay?" A young man asked worriedly. Forgetting I was sitting in church, I nodded "Yes," slightly ashamed of the torrential outpour of tears streaming down my cheeks.

"Do you need me to get someone for you?" he inquired. "No, I will be okay. I will talk with the pastor after."

"Okay," he replied.

I could hear the relief in his voice. For so many years, I had buried the horrifying shame of my past, hoping never to have to deal with it, but after rededicating my life to God, this dreaded secret was rearing its ugly head. The pain I had been carrying had weighed me down in the pit of self-loathing, bitterness, anger, and grief for my stolen childhood.

That Sabbath, like most, I sat and listened intently to the sermon, and I could not hold back my tears. My bitter cup had reached its capacity and was running over. The poison that had lined the pit of my life was seeping into my soul, and I felt I was drowning; I could not save myself.

I was tired of being angry all the time. The pain had altered my life and left me empty and full all at the same time. I had tried everything! I overworked and explored every self-indulgent vice, from compulsive shopping, neurotic eating, drinking, promiscuity, and self-harm. Then finally, when all else failed, I started praying honestly and desperately. I was trying to get a quick fix for my problem, but disappointingly, I was coming up empty. Nothing could fill the void or erase the pain. I suffered in silence for many years, and after giving my life to God, I thought He would erase the pain immediately. Little did I know that God was taking me through a painful process of waiting for my healing and deliverance.

"How dare you? How dare you tell me that this all-seeing, all-knowing, all-loving, and caring God would allow a child to endure such horrific pain for His glory? How is it possible that He can see everything yet did nothing to stop it? Was He so busy saving the Universe that He had forgotten me? I was a child, for goodness' sake." I glared at the pastor, who had extended his hand to take mine at the front door after his sermon. I yelled at him with trembling lips, a cracked voice, snorting nose, and a rivulet of tears streaming down my pain-stricken face.

Pit of Self-Sabotage

The little girl trapped in a woman's body screamed for help. "Please explain to me why I have to carry this pain, hurt, shame, and guilt around?" My outburst shocked me, but I could not help myself. Some members briskly walked by, not wanting to disturb the awkward commotion.

Seeing my distress and distorted appearance, the frightened pastor quickly escorted me to the vestibule. He offered me a seat, pulled up a chair, and sat beside me. I was weeping uncontrollably, not caring what I looked like. The pain I felt was unbearable, and I needed someone to help me get rid of it. He handed me his handkerchief and waited for me to calm down.

"What happened to you?" He asked with concern and sincerity.

"My, my ahmm, oh God, my ahmm, father raped me when I was a child. I was only eleven when he first tried, and then again when I was thirteen. I tried fighting him off as best as possible, but he was much stronger." I lowered my voice, shocked that I had just blurted out all that information. "He took my innocence!" I spoke through clenched teeth. "He took my pride, joy, and peace, and I cannot get it back. I will never get it back. Why!? Why would God allow my father to do that?"

I looked away, afraid and ashamed to see his eyes. The tears began to flow even more rapidly as I realized the words that were sputtering from my mouth. I had never shared that information with anyone. My stepmother had instructed me to take it to my grave, a grave that seemed too far away. I wrapped my arms around myself, feeling naked and exposed, but I couldn't stop.

The reservoir of my soul was brimming, bulging, and bursting, and I couldn't hold the liquid frustration in anymore.

"At fourteen years old, I had to decide whether to carry my father's child or to get rid of it. He made me into a murderer!" I sobbed, burying my head in my hands, and wept even more. I desperately wanted to be freed, but my shame bound me in a contortion of pain. The pastor was silent. I could tell he was also hurting because he started weeping with me. "I am so sorry," he muttered with a trembling voice. "I am so, so, sorry that happened to you. I can't imagine the pain you must have gone through, but God understands."

"Where was He? Where was He?" I screamed in anger. "Why didn't He save me?" I looked at the pastor, hoping to find an answer.

"I don't know, my child, I don't know."

A knock could be heard at the door.

"Yes?" The pastor tried to change his tone.

"Your lunch is ready, sir."

"Yes, thank you. Can you put it up for me?"

Who could eat at a time like this? I thought to myself.

"Okay," came the reply.

Returning his attention to me, "What is your name?"

"It is Carlene," I replied.

"Carlene," he sounded direct, "I don't know why God did not step in and help you right then and there, but I know for sure that God does not make mistakes. He loves you and would not bring you through something if He cannot fix it. When I say that God allows things to happen for His glory, I mean He wants you to turn your pain and sorrow over to Him. He can take your pain and turn it into joy, but you must allow Him. Carlene, I think the Lord has a plan for you, and you may not see it now, but He may bring you to a place where this pain will be no more."

I listened as the pastor tried to tell me of God's amazing goodness for me, but his attempt did not convince me. I needed proof, and he did not have it to give.

He shared the horrific story of his niece. He and his family were having lunch at church when they heard a scream from the church balcony. They discovered that someone had gotten into the church and raped his six-year-old niece, playing on the balcony, and then tried to push her off it. I stopped breathing and looked at him.

"What!?" I exclaimed. "So, how can you still trust God?" I asked with unrestraint anger.

He paused and looked at me. "It hurts; it really hurts when I think about my innocent little niece. She will never be the same. I was mad at God for doing nothing for a while, but I still believe He loves my niece and has a plan for her."

We both sat in silence for a while. After he prayed for me, I walked away that evening, determined in my heart that I needed to hear from the Lord.

That night, I told the Lord in no uncertain terms that I needed proof that He was real, and that He loved me beyond unreasonable doubt. I told him I would not pray or attend church until He proved He was real. "I am done!" I looked up and pointed to the sky to ensure I had His attention. "I am done playing church; I am done pretending everything is alright with me. I am done!" I repeated. "I don't understand, so make me understand how a loving God could be so busy attending to other things while a helpless child was violated and tarnished in such a heinous way." My mind was made up. I needed proof. That night I held my pillow and wept bitterly.

* * *

"Find something; you need to find something. No one walks away from a head-on collision without injury or internal bleeding; find something."

"Why are you shouting?" I muttered with great effort, trying to wake from my sleep. "Oh, ooooh!" I screamed in pain as I came to consciousness. *What's going on? Where am I? Why am I hurting so much? Why are there so many people in white coats? What happened?* I tried to look around but was restricted by the brace around my neck and the restraint across my body.

"Ms. Faulknor, you were in an accident. You are at the Kings County Hospital." I heard in the distance while I was wheeled away to a dark room for more testing.

I must have drifted off again because I heard someone asking me a question in the distance.

Pit of Self-Sabotage

"Is this proof enough for you?"

"What, who is that?" I tried to turn, but the restraints prevented me from moving.

"Where am I?" I asked sleepily, opening my eyes, and realizing that I was in a different room. This room had nothing. It was quiet, and all the hustle and bustling before had stopped. This felt different, peaceful. The room was completely white, and the atmosphere was indescribable. Almost as if I was floating on water.

"Is this proof enough for you?" The voice seemed to come closer.

"Proof? What are you talking about?"

I wondered who this person was and why His voice sounded like a quiet spring in my ears. I was confused for a moment. I remember getting dressed that morning and making my favorite breakfast: salt-fish fritters and hominy corn porridge. I even remembered my father comparing my cooking to my grandfather's. My precious Tata's cooking, "Nothing can compare to that," I told him and then left the house for work. Laying there, I saw flashes of a movie in the distance. I saw what appeared to be a traffic accident replaying in slow motion. I saw myself behind the wheel of my car, trying desperately to control it after drastically swerving away from an approaching vehicle. Unfortunately, my car could not endure that drastic swerve but spiraled uncontrollably toward the two-lane oncoming traffic. *Death is inevitable*, I thought in a flash as I canvassed the area for an escape. I stared hopelessly at my last moments. The first car was coming directly at me and would hit me in the second car, snuffing out my life.

In the distance, I saw a face laughing hysterically, mockingly, and jarringly.

"Yes, I got you now!"

I knew right away that it was Satan celebrating my demise.

"Pray!" a voice commanded, distracting me from the face that was laughing.

"No, it's too late," I replied, partly because I had told the Lord I would not pray anymore, and I was refusing to give in.

"Pray!" the voice said again.

It's too late!" I responded.

"Pray!" The voice sounded desperate and directed the third time.

"Je---s," was the only thing I could remember saying. I saw the most humongous hand reaching down in the middle of my car, scooping me up to safety. In that instant, I was rescued from the pit of death.

"Oh! Oh," tears began to flow, "you saved me." Realizing at that moment the Lord himself had come to my rescue.

"Why would you do that? Why?" I wept bitterly.

I was glad He saved me, but I became angry when I remembered the pain, shame, and guilt that bound me.

Pit of Self-Sabotage

"You should have just let me die. Why didn't you let me die?"

"I could not let you die," came the sweet voice. "I had to prove to you that I love you and that I have always been with you. I have never left your side since the day you were born. Every pain, hurt, and disappointment, I was there holding you and drying your tears. I have never left you. You are loved, my child, chosen and handpicked because I have a plan for your life if you only trust my leading."

I felt a calm peace that I had never felt before. My tears were now like raindrops washing away all my pain. At that moment, my Savior took my hands in His and lovingly healed my broken heart. I tried to tell Him I was damaged, but He told me He could restore and replace what the Devil had stolen from me. I told him I was robbed of my innocence, and He told me not to worry as He had replaced all that was taken. This was the day my Lord and I started a new relationship.

He reminded me that I was chosen and handpicked to help others who suffered as I did. He told me that He knew me before I was even knitted in my mother's womb and that I was not a mistake. Oh, the words sounded like music to my ears. I wanted to leap off my bed and skip around like a little girl singing, "He loves me! Oh, how He loves me so."

It was at that moment the Lord told me so much about myself. He told me how special I was to Him. He laid it on my heart that I needed to go back to school and study ministry. Like Sarah, I laughed at Him. "Are you serious, Lord? Do you remember who I am? How could I get into ministry? I am damaged goods. Have you forgotten that they said I was not smart enough for school? Or have you forgotten I don't even have a high school diploma?" He smiled and asked if anything was impossible with Him. This was the day I started the painful restoration process in His divine pit. For years I felt I was waiting on God to deliver me. It turns out that God was waiting for me to surrender and release the poison of lies that held me in the pit of self-sabotage.

Who could it be but the Lord? I tried to rationalize my encounter. *Was it a dream? If it was a dream, why did I feel so free? The tightness and ache in my chest were gone. If it was just a dream, how would He know how to answer me and say the right things? Am I going crazy? What will people say when I tell them I had an encounter with the Lord? Afraid of what others would think, I kept my encounter to myself and returned to life as usual.*

But life was never the same again. A spirit of depression consumed and permeated my soul. I descended into a pit of extreme promiscuity and suicidal ideation. I felt as though all the force of hell moved in with me and my life began spiraling out of control. My prayer life became non-existent, and I felt God had gone completely silent. To make matters worse, things at home became more intense with my father and stepmother, with whom I was now living after migrating to the United States. I had left their home at the age of sixteen to escape physical, verbal, and mental abuse but here I was living in the same dysfunctional home I escaped from years before.

Somehow, I was under the impression that my family had changed and that the years that passed between us had brought clarity and repentance. Instead, I faced the hard reality that little had changed with them, except now I was an independent working woman they

Pit of Self-Sabotage

could no longer whip. However, I was still the black sheep in the family, and my precious daughter also seemed to inherit that position. The desire to kill them grew more intense, but I could not pull it off. Sometimes I came close to driving a knife into my stepmother or father's neck, but something kept getting in the way. This intensified my pain and hatred toward them.

Even after that encounter with God, I felt as though I was being dragged back into a dark pit again. I constantly cried, unable to control my emotions. I was consumed with guilt, hate, bitterness, and shame. Every day was dark and gloomy; it seemed like it rained only on my side of the fence.

Desperate, I prayed again, asking God to constantly remove the dark clouds that hovered over me, but He seemed silent. I wanted desperately to hear that sweet voice again, the One that told me I was special and that I was wanted. Rather, I was tormented by the voices telling me I was not good enough and would never measure up. Telling me I was damaged and irreparable.

The more I prayed, the more I felt condemned and alone. I concluded that I had gone too far in sin to be redeemed. Drowning in my mess and shame, living became a nightmare for me. Waking up to the realization that I was still alive completely drained me. Death became my only desire.

One morning around 3a.m, in one of my desperate pleas for God to take away the darkness that engulfed me, I heard His voice again. It was clear and precise; there was no hesitation or question. "The only way for you to be free from the shame and pain you carry is to go to your father and tell him that you have forgiven him and that he needs to forgive himself too."

"What? Are you serious? Are you out of your mind? How dare you tell me to forgive him? I want to kill that scum bag. I hate him! I hate him!" I yelled. and cursed at the voice. I said some words that I could not repeat here. "I will not tell him that! I will not! He does not deserve my forgiveness. Never! I will never forgive him!"

For days I was mad at God for asking me to give up my poisoned pain through forgiveness. Adamant and convinced that I knew best about my situation, I walked out of the conversation determined to hold on to the pain.

This new encounter with the Lord left me feeling betrayed. Why would the Lord ask me to do such a thing? Did He forget all the things I had endured? Why would I want to forgive this good-for-nothing man? He took my innocence, pride, joy, and life. When I forgive him, what will happen to me? What will I have left? I grew even more resentful towards the Lord.

Looking back now, I realize that at that point, all the demons left hell and took up residence in my home. I went with anyone who would give me attention, and then I would mock God and tell Him it was all his fault. "Why don't you stop me?" I shook my fist toward the sky, staggering to get to my apartment, not from drunkenness but under the invisible load of pain that was too heavy for me to carry.

One morning after I awoke and realized I was still alive; I emptied and swallowed a bottle of sleeping pills. Unfortunately, I had to

Pit of Self-Sabotage

call my work to tell my boss I was not coming in. Realizing that something was wrong, he kept questioning me because I had work.

Later that night, I jumped in my car and drove through all the red lights with my eyes closed hoping someone would hit me. A friend called and demanded I meet up with him. I spent the night weeping on his shoulders. I wanted someone to rescue me, but nobody seemed to care. All everyone saw was my bubbly personality, my fake smile, and my well-dressed apparel, but no one bothered to look into my eyes to see the pain. I was a disaster waiting to happen, a volatile volcano waiting to explode.

Several days later, in the stillness of the night, He spoke again. "You want to be free?" He asked. "Yes, I do, please take this darkness away!" I desperately pleaded.

"Go to your father and tell him you have forgiven him and that he needs to forgive himself." Then it was silence again. I was too tired to fight so I hugged my body and drifted off to sleep. The following day defiantly, I told the Lord I would never forgive my father and that He needed to just forget about it. Several weeks later, I received a call from a university in Fort Lauderdale, Florida, inviting me to interview for a job I did not apply for. After several miraculous events, I got the job and was ready to move from New York to Florida to start a new life.

When I went to say my goodbyes to my family, everyone except my father was sitting around in the living room. When I asked where he was, I was told he was in the bedroom. I walked into the room without hesitation, like someone was leading me. I sat on

Waiting In the Pit

the bed next to him, something I had never done before, and told him that I forgave him and that he needed to forgive himself. He sat straight up in the bed and looked at me as if he saw a ghost. I went on to tell him that I loved him. He responded, "I love you too, my daughter." I hugged my father (I had never hugged my father before) and walked out of the room. No! I floated out of the room. Immediately, a peace I had never felt before flooded my body, and I felt free for the first time.

I ascended out of the pit I had languished in for years. I felt the poison that threatened to consume my soul diluting and dissipating. The loads I was carrying were lifted off, and I was floating. When I got back to the living room, everyone was staring at me with a puzzled look. "What happened?" my stepmother asked.

"Oh, I just told my dad I forgave him."

"What?" She stammered as tears welled up in her eyes. She picked up her phone and dialed my sister, who lived in Virginia. I heard screams and laughter. She pointed at my face and told me I was glowing.

I touched my cheeks, once stained with tears, and felt the radiance of my smile stretching across my face. I did not understand the magnitude of my appearance until my baby girl, and I walked down the stairs. She kept looking at me strangely. When I asked her why she was looking at me like that, she related that my face was bright. My face was bright indeed.

For the first time in my life, I saw colors outside and the sun's brightness. The woman who walked into the house was a completely different woman from the one who walked out. All I can say is praise be to the Lord.

I wish I had obeyed the Lord when He told me to forgive. I would have been free months before. Even the food I eat now tastes better. Waking each day is a delight and joy to my soul. Life has now become meaningful and delightful. I no longer want to take my life or self-harm, nor do I ever feel like drowning in a dark hole of shame and guilt. I am free because Jesus told me I was free, and who the Son sets free is free indeed. After years of suffering and waiting in my pit of self-sabotage, deliverance came through forgiveness, and I am now FREE!

Meet Carlene Francis

Carlene Francis is a preacher, counselor, entrepreneur, aspiring spiritual leader and trauma-informed speaker. She holds a master's degree in social work and youth ministry.

Carlene is a very resourceful and passionate woman of God. She is the founder of "Healing the Source," a platform where she talks about trauma, and "Son's Flowers," a nonprofit geared at helping young people learn life skills such as cooking, sewing, arts and crafts, and furniture reupholstering. Carlene shares her life story in her two-part series: *The Wounded Bird* and *The Wounded Bird Still Flies.*

CHAPTER 3

Saved In the Pit

"And after my skin has been destroyed, yet in my flesh I will see God; I myself will I see him with my own eyes I, and not another. How my heart yearns within me!" **Job 19:26-27 (NIV)**

As a child, I hardly ever fell ill. I have no recollection of even having the common cold. My childhood was not entirely pleasant as I faced many hardships such as poverty, homelessness, and hunger—you name it, I have lived it. However, ill health was never a part of my track record. Yes, I have sustained many injuries, cuts, and bruises, but the usual sniffles and viruses that typically plague children didn't visit me. They must have been planning and plotting to make a grand debut later in my life.

As for cuts and bruises, I was the child that did not understand that if a bicycle was heading in my direction while walking on the road, the safest stance was to stay still. For some reason, I always succeeded in confusing the rider with my sudden movements and then suffered the consequences afterward. I can remember after each collision; these cyclists would ask, "Why did you move?" After each episode, I always walked away from these collisions with scratches and bruises and a swollen face. I learned to be my own nurse to patch up my scrapes, so a little self-care and a cup of mom's sugar and water concoction always got me up and running again.

But then I turned twenty-eight (28) years old, and my impeccable health records was suddenly tarnished. As I knew it, life was about to take a drastic turn. Having just completed my college education, I was optimistic about my future. I was ready to leave the "patty shop" job I held for seven years, and I now wanted to graze the fields of the corporate world. Little did I know that the All-Knowing, All-Seeing, All-Powerful God, the Great I Am, had other plans for me ahead.

At twenty-eight (28) years old, I did not know who Jesus was. I had attended church many times and heard the Gospel preached several times, but I did not know anything about God. Although I was not an avid partygoer or outgoing person, I was oblivious to who Jesus was and did not care to know Him then. I had no clue I would need a Savior, a Healer, and a Deliverer.

In August of 2011, I started feeling a tingling sensation all over my body. I did not think much of it, as it was the summer season. I attributed this feeling to the intensity of the heat that defined that summer season. Even though I was conscious of this new sensation, it was not a big deal and incited no alarm. Shortly after making this observation, the joint and muscle pains arrived. They took root in every corner and crevice of my body where muscles were present, and they came with aggression. Immediately following, I realized that my mobility had started to diminish. Something as simple as getting out of bed suddenly became a struggle. Stooping, walking briskly, getting in and out of motor vehicles, taking a shower or bath, or even playing with and lifting my six-year-old son had all become a chore for me. Instead of lifting him, I asked my son to stand on my back as I desperately sought to ease the relentless pain coursing through my back. All the activities that were once normal for me became almost impossible. Naturally, this evoked concern and alarm and gave more than enough reason to visit the doctor. Remember, before this, illness was a foreigner to me. I did not know how to process or bear all of this.

The doctor's appointment came, then the tests, then the results. According to the doctors, by all indications, I was developing rheumatic arthritis. They reported that I was displaying all the signs of this medical condition. The only problem was the test results did not align with their prognosis. All results came back negative. I was prescribed painkillers just to try and negate the constant pain that I was feeling, but the pain would not die.

While I was busy grappling with that, my skin started to discolor. Now I had to seek the opinion of a dermatologist. Upon my arrival, she examined my skin and concluded that I had severe seborrheic dermatitis. Again, I was prescribed medications, and again, none of them worked. As if I wasn't dealing with enough medical problems, another terrible condition joined the parade. I noticed that any touch to my skin was excruciating, particularly on my face and fingers. Upon closer inspection, I noticed boils erupting all over my face. The boils later opened and oozed a puslike substance and left sores. Only God knew the horror I endured watching my face mutate into a sore field. I felt as if my entire world had come to an end. I had excruciating pains in my joints and muscles, and the sores were unbelievably agonizing. They littered my face from ear to ear and all my fingers. Surprisingly, the sores developed into craters on my face and arms. Something within these sores was eating at my very flesh!

At this point, the pain and discomfort I was undergoing was unspeakable. As you can imagine, I had to take a break from work and desperately sought relief by visiting all the major hospitals in Jamaica. They conducted many tests and concluded that besides having rheumatic arthritis and seborrheic dermatitis, I now had discoid lupus! One doctor even recommended that I do a biopsy on my face. That day, I cried so hard and ran out of the hospital. I got so frustrated after listening to all those doctors' speculations and vain recommendations. Again, the results did not confirm any of these diagnoses. They explained that it was not unusual for the results to be contrary to what the symptoms dictated.

In addition to me living through all those mentioned above, my right arm and some of my fingers swiftly became deformed. They could no longer stretch out! Did I also mention that the mysterious illness had reduced me to my skeletal frame? Oh yes, it did; I went from a size six to a size zero. I was skin and bones.

I was in this invasive pit bumping from one sub-pit to another. I was in a pit of pain, a pit of skin discoloration, the pit of deformity, the pit of sores; even the craters became literal pits on my body! I noticed people's expressions; I could hear their chatter when they saw me. Knowing Jamaicans, I can imagine them assuming I had full-blown AIDS considering my appearance. People who saw me would look at me and cringe.

In my Job-like affliction, I must testify that I did not have the type of friends Job had. God blessed me with a solid support system. My family members still rallied around and helped in whatever area they could; I greatly appreciate this. Even with the raw smell that accompanied my putrid sores and my ghastly appearance, they treated me well and comforted me in the best way they could. But there is one friend who gave me more than comforting words. She encouraged me to visit her church to obtain prayer. I went, and they prayed earnestly for me. I later felt what I know to be a conviction in my heart. I had to answer the call to come to Jesus.

On that fateful day of March 12, 2012, I walked into a pool and got baptized. Before that, I had a serious talk with the Lord. I told Him I was going down in the water with sores and craters, but that was the end. I felt like I was going down in the river Jordan, and even if my miracle may not be as dramatic as Naaman's, I needed a miracle! I declared in His name that no more sores and craters would surface on my skin, and the ones there would dry up and disappear forever. The Lord Jesus heard, and He answered my prayers. After a while, the sore and craters dried up. Hallelujah! But all the other issues remained and persisted for four years. During this time, my doctors placed me on steroids which eased the pain and helped with the skin discoloration, facial swelling, weakness, and fatigue.

By the end of 2012, I was able to travel to Canada for work. I traveled in March of 2013. About a year in, I realized I had become too dependent on these steroids for my functionality. I believed more in those medications than in my Jehovah Rapha. I felt convicted in my heart that the Lord was saying to me, "Trust Me." The Holy Spirit who dwells within helped me to muster up the courage I needed to rid myself of this bondage of drug dependency. One day, I picked them up and headed to the bathroom. I threw them into the toilet and then flushed them. This felt so liberating; I was finally wholly surrendering, giving the Lord complete control over my life. Like a rabbit in springtime, I popped my nose up from my pit, smelling fresh air for the first time.

About a year on, all the symptoms, except for the deformity, sores, and craters, resurfaced! Only, this time they did not come alone. They came with a more obnoxious assailant. My hair started to fall out rapidly, my God! It came out in chunks at a time, without any form of new growth in sight. This continued until I was almost entirely bald. Wigs and heavy makeup became the veils behind which I hid the shame and the embarrassing reality of my appearance. My scalp was now itching ceaselessly. Ask me about being tormented in your body; I have experienced it first-hand.

By this time, I had returned to see the doctor in the province where I stayed. After examining me, he realized my case was more than he could handle. This doctor documented all his findings and gave them to me to take to a dermatologist he recommended in Edmonton. When I saw the piles of paper with his supposed diagnosis, I said, "Lord, you are in control."

The time came for me to visit the dermatologist. He read through the referral and then began his assessment. This doctor proceeded to withdraw approximately ten test tubes of blood from my feeble body, all in the name of running multiple tests. He also conducted heart, lung, and kidney tests (to name a few). All those test results came back ... yes, you guessed it, negative!

I was choking in this excessively dark, haunting pit of symptoms, drowning from the endless tears I cried day and night. There were days when I asked the Lord to please take my life rather than allow me to waste away in this pit of a body. I was prescribed products for my skin and scalp, but nothing worked. I did not know what else to do or pray. By this, I had watched all the healing testimonies on YouTube, including the miraculous healing testimony of recording Gospel artist Glacia Robinson. I also read all the Scriptures that spoke of healing in the Bible.

I knew He could heal me. I knew He was always willing to heal. I could not understand why He took so long to pull me out of my horrible pit, even though He extended grace, and sustained me to work and function through it all. It could have only been Him. Looking back, I know it had to be because my physical flesh was failing me, yet I survived.

I can remember an incident while going to work one winter afternoon. On my path, I had to go down a few park stairs; these were large steps, all covered in snow. I attempted to take the first step, but my legs failed, and my frail frame fell flat. I lay there on my back and cried. I said, *"God, why are You allowing me to endure all this pain? I am not old, yet my entire being is working against me."* I stayed there and cried for about ten minutes, struggled to pull myself up, brushed the snow off, thanked the Lord, and then continued my journey to work.

Waiting In the Pit

It was now May 2015, and I had ended my contract. I traveled back to Jamaica for the first time after two years. Being away from my son, family, and friends was difficult, and I was happy to reunite with them. Even though the problems persisted, I felt a sense of happiness for the first time in two years just by being in their presence. At this point, my body became immune to all the pit experiences. The image of my original features was almost completely erased from my recollection. I had to revisit pictures I had taken to understand who and what I looked like. Of course, I did not do this often, as I usually have bitter/sweet reactions each time. Bitter because my present look was that of an old woman and sweet in that I hoped the Lord would change my story and restore me through His healing.

I tried as much as possible to keep my eyes on the Lord while waiting in my pits of affliction, despair, and sorrow. The Lord Jesus shifted my focus. He needed all of me, all my heart, mind, body, and soul. I started to worship differently. I started having sweet communion with the Holy Spirit and intimacy with Christ Jesus.

In August 2015, exactly four years after illness held me hostage; I had a dream one night. I dreamt I was among people who accused me of a crime I knew nothing of. I tried pleading my innocence with them, but they would not have it. They insisted that I was guilty of the crime. One of them pulled out a firearm, put it to my head then pulled the trigger. After receiving that bullet to my head, I fell to the ground. I felt the breath leaving my body. I was dying! But then, miraculously, the Lord healed my wound and blew back the breath into me. I stood up again amid all of them. They were shocked that I was still alive but were adamant that I must die! They proclaimed, "You must die today, today!"

Two of them held my arms, dragged me to an area with a wooden fenced cage, and locked me inside. They all chanted, "Yes, kill her! She must die!" I stood in the caged pit, waiting to see what they would do next. They started throwing lit gas bombs over the top of the fence. They all fell inside the cage because there was no roof to block them. As these bombs hit the ground near me, they burst into flames. The flames became unbearable until I collapsed in pain and exhaustion.

I was dying once more. My eyes dimmed shut, and I was about to take my last breath. Then, I felt someone holding onto my left hand. When I opened my eyes, I saw an angel! He smiled at me and said, "It will be ok." Almost immediately, I felt someone holding my right hand as well. I turned to see another angel who said the same thing. Both angels spoke, but their lips did not move. I could hear what they were saying in my mind. I smiled and nodded at them.

They lifted me and flew with me in the air hovering over the top of the fence. All the people on the other side of the wall looked on in amazement, their mouths wide open. The angels were invisible to them, so they thought I was flying. The angels placed me among them. As soon as my feet touched the ground, I began to speak in my heavenly language. They continued to look on in perplexity. They could not understand why or how I was still alive, or why I was still breathing. They hung their heads in shame and walked away from me, and I woke up. Hallelujah!

Following that supernatural dream, I felt the death edict leave my body. All my symptoms started to dissipate. My hair started growing back, the pains left my body, the actual color of my skin started to seep through the discoloration, and I began to regain weight. I questioned the Lord. I asked, "Lord, why did you allow this illness to last for four good years?" He answered, "My daughter, I was always willing to heal you, but I was more interested in saving you. I needed to get you to that place where I was solely in control of your heart." Right there and then, I understood that God saved me in my pit. Through Him saving me, I experienced the fullness of Him, who fills all in all.

I tasted and felt death clawing for my soul. My flesh, muscles, and joints were rotting away, but like Job, I will declare:

"And after my skin has been destroyed, yet in my flesh I will see God; I myself will I see him with my own eyes I, and not another. How my heart yearns within me!" Job 19:26-27 (NIV)

I still have scars on my fingers and even over the top of my eyes. I call them my badges of honor; a testament to my endurance and God's mercy. They are reminders that God is a healer. When others shower compliments on me, saying, "You look so young; you don't look anything like your age!" I always answer, "It's only because of the grace of God."

Meet Tashina Morrison

Tashina S. Morrison is a saved, sanctified, and Holy Ghost-filled woman of God. She hails from the tropical island of Jamaica. She is the mother of a brilliant young man.

Tashina is a banker who also dabbles in dress-making. Cooking is one of her favorite pastimes; she enjoys creating new dishes. She takes pleasure in serving the Lord through the usher ministry at her church, Linstead Pentecostal Tabernacle.

After reading her chapter, she desires that souls will come to know Jesus Christ. She has many stories that embody the miraculous works of God and plans to expand her writing.

Her mantra is Philippians 4:13 "I can do all things through Christ who strengthens me."

CHAPTER 4

The Bi-sexual Woman at the Well

"Come, see a man, which told me all things that ever I did: is not this the Christ? **(John 4:29)"**

In John 4:2-26, John recounts the ball-by-ball encounter of a woman bound by sexual immorality, imprisoned by the gossip of her community, and enslaved by her sinful desire. This woman had five husbands, and the one she had presently was not her own to flaunt. She needed water to drink, cook, clean, and wash but was too ashamed to fetch it amongst the other women and villagers. She was scorned by many and suffered from extreme self-condemnation. Yet, Prince Emmanuel, "who must go through Samaria" (John 4:4), intentionally "sat thus on the well" (John 4:6) waiting for that Samaritan woman. She was about to come face to face with a man who intimately knew about her, a knowledge that others shamed her for while only having bits and pieces of information. He, the Way, the Truth, and the Life, would embrace her so deeply that the redemptive love would restore her with great expediency.

Like the woman at the well, I too, was bound by a sexual vice called same-sex attraction and action. I was imprisoned by the comments and perceptions of others and enslaved by a broken heart. I needed my heart to be mended, freed from the lust of the flesh, and no longer be captive to condemnation. At the well of mercy and forgiveness, Jesus met me. He knew the intimate details which a few tried to bake hops bread out of the crumbs of their knowledge. His arms embraced and comforted me. Like the woman at the well, this chapter is my running to the community of believers to say, "Come see a man who told me all that I ever did. Can this be the Christ?" (John 4:29 ESV)

We met at a church function. I was presenting, and at some point during the day, our paths crossed. I sensed the immediate mutual attraction; kindred spirits with a "back road." The ease of communication, the flirting, the electrical charges in the stomach when she passed by, and the sexual moisture of being close to her were too palpable to ignore. Making her laugh was easy. She knew just what to say to have my twenty-eight teeth reflecting the brightness of the day. (*pause*) "Dear Father, please hold my heart." (*unpause*) We exchanged numbers that day. How could I not ask? How could she not say yes? I smiled all the way back home. I couldn't wait to message her.

It took a few days before I messaged. I was doing an online class then, and she came to mind. The blushing and flirtatious feeling quickly osmotized throughout my body. Like a magnet to the ferromagnetic material, my fingers pulled at my cell phone and began the line that would ignite our romantic relationship. I messaged, "I'm doing schoolwork but need a distraction." The sails of the venereal ship were hoisted, the breeze of mutual desirability blew, and the waters of seduction moved us in a steady forward motion. We were sailing to our first physical destination, where words transformed into action. To find someone whose mind has depth and insight is a natural attraction for me.

Every interaction was choreographed with seamless poise and rapture. You see, we both met each other at a time when heterosexual love had failed, hurt, lied, and cheated. We were both mature in our professional lives; emotionally, we wanted romance and enjoyment; spiritually, we were quite active and involved in the church; and sexually, we were chaste yet willing to explore something different. That first night in the privacy of the well-painted walls, I made my first move, which was readily welcomed. Like seeds to fertile ground, our weekly conversations before that weekend now hung succulently ripe on the branch of carnal intimacy. I was the farmer, and she was the soft, edible fruit. From that moment, we became inseparable.

Let me pause here to say the sexual relationship was wrong. It was immoral and against God's principles. However, our romantic relationship, love, and heartbreak were real.

A distinct encounter that added fuel to the path of same-sex attraction was a novel written by a black American author who told a romantic story of a heterosexual couple. There were problems with the heterosexual couple and the girlfriend sought mesmerized refuge from this intelligent, attractive, and engaging feminine black woman. The words of the book sparked an interest that I wanted to explore.

The Bible is true; "by beholding, we are changed." (2 Corinthians 3:18) By beholding those images, I was changing into a lifestyle that causes angels to hide their faces. Whilst the book shaped the course of the type of woman I was sexually attracted to, it was not the cause or turning point that let me not feel safe as a girl. At a young age I was molested. As a teenager I encountered a few sexual assaults. Sexual trauma may not be spoken of by mouth, but the mind and body relive it.

A church member messaged me to warn me about my closeness with this young lady and that I needed to stop what I was doing with her. Man was I scared and hopping mad all at once. Afraid that I would be found out and hopping mad because *Who is she to come to talk about my sin? Check your house frè.* (Brother in French Creole). Oh, how well we defensively deflect when Christ uses others to save us from our sins. May I add that this church member began to connect the dots because a friend who knew about me and this young lady left evidence of breadcrumbs. Therefore, I was also mad at my friend. I laugh as I recount this part of the story. My "breadcrumbs" friend was at a point in her life where hiding was no longer an option; if this is where you are, this is where you are.

The next upset between her and me was the guilt train. It was getting noisier. At that point, instead of hopping off the train, I relinquished myself of active duty to my Lord and Savior. I hopped off the Jesus train. I reasoned with Matthew 6:24, "One cannot serve two masters." Right? You will love one and hate the other. I honestly thought that I could have done it. Please believe I loved Jesus; every mission work was done with my whole heart. The truth was this relationship was the undercurrent of my walk with God. After rationalizing the matter, the battle between the carnal and the spiritual man ensued. Like the claws of a lion, the carnal foe tore through the sensibilities of the spiritual and took full reign over the grasslands of my heart.

We had no secrets, as we were each other's confidants. We spoke about it, laughed, and decided not to let that deter us. I must reiterate that when we met each other, we were both walking with the Lord. Our divine purpose was to strengthen each other's walk as iron sharpens iron. Satan, however, knew that we both had forbidden interests that would dull each other's spiritual sword and launched his temptation rockets accordingly.

She was a great support to me. She knew how to listen, was encouraging, and helped me be more organized. The reciprocity of this relationship was breathtaking. However, the time had come for us to be physically separated as a couple. When we met, she was in a heterosexual relationship that was heading "south" real fast. When that relationship ended, I was ready to be open about our love, a love that brought mutual happiness, a love that felt like home. I was ready to marry her. Sadly, she was not ready to be open; she wasn't ready for the shock and condemnation that would come from family and friends. She wanted us to remain "in the closet." At that moment, I felt utterly rejected. But our relationship continued.

A new year was approaching, and the guilt train returned with the rejected feeling. The train came with increased intensity, steam, and speed. I couldn't do it anymore. The "no" to my open relationship and the guilt of telling others about the love of Jesus while I was in love with a woman could no longer co-exist. I had to choose a side. I had to end this gnawing feeling. So, I called my confidant. It was very late when I called her, so she knew something was wrong. I told her my ordeal of guilt. I told her I didn't want to lose her and still wanted her in my life, not as a lover but as a friend. There was silence. There was a flood of tears for us both. There was more silence. Then, there was an end to our romantic relationship.

Our friendship continued. We would still talk as before, minus romance, and sexual pleasures. Until that day. That day, I felt a nudge in my stomach. I knew something was off. I could not shake that feeling. I suspected what it was, but God knows I was not ready for the world of hurt that was about to come upon me. With much hesitation and knots in my stomach, I asked her, and she answered. She had found someone else. She was now in a heterosexual relationship. Around that time, I wanted us to get back together, and she kept saying no. Her argument, which was solid, was because of the reality of how sad I would be when we were intimate. What would change? In those conversations, I realized I was ready to be with her knowing full well the eternal cost and loss.

Her relationship with the young man continued. And with every passing day, I felt like I was disintegrating. I remember another request for us to get back together. This time it was after an event of the unknown for many. When I asked her, her reply solidified that my request would never be met. She confessed that if she had died during that catastrophe, she was not certain where her eternity would lie. So, she was choosing heaven.

Yup. Yup. For the next two weeks, I was a mirror reflection of shattered pieces of glass that constantly cut at my heart. My mattress was my casket, the pillows were my sorrowful rest, and my sheet was a body-length wreath. Sleep was the abiding grim reaper that taunted my present situation. Quiet moments were filled with thoughts of her. Satan, the adversary of my soul, did all that he could to brace me against the wall of shame and chokehold me with guilt. He intended to squeeze my life out so I would lose all hope. But, like the woman at the well, who came for water when no one was around, Jesus was sitting and waiting for me to come; He was waiting for me to thirst; He was waiting for me to go for a drink of water. At my well of shame, guilt, and heartache. The One who has my name engraved in the palm of His hand held my heart in His nail-pierced hands. Even after disappointing Him, my Maker still wanted me.

Psalm 139:8 "...if I make my bed in hell, behold, thou art there."

My Father, my husband Jesus, my comforting Holy Spirit, and my best friend, my guardian angel, would **NOT** allow the enemy to win. When Christ hung on that cross "Totani" (*Naked in French Creole*) He hung for me.

Like clay slabbed onto the circular plinth, in the adept hand of the Potter, Christ Jesus. The centrifugal force of forgiveness and healing shaped the ball clay of my renewed spiritual vows between I and my Isaiah 54:5 Husband. The remodeling of my life began. There was work that I needed to do. Jesus wants us to be co-

The Bi-sexual Woman at the Well

laborers with Him for the sanctification of our souls. My work was to call her and ask that we not speak anymore. For me to heal, I had to cut ties with her. I had to experience not talking to her, not hearing her voice, and not getting comfort from her. I had to experience not sharing my laughs with her. I had to stand alone but stand alone with Christ.

A well is a pit where the thirsty come to draw water from. The sexual assaults and the romantic book were both the wormhole and the escalator that lowered me into my pit of indiscretion. But Jesus sat on the pit/well of hope to quench my thirst for the lust of the flesh. Let me take a moment to share with you the divine intimacy that Christ revealed to me. A romantic partner is one I would spend time with; one I would call morning, noon, and night; one I would plan dates with; one I would talk about with blushes; one I would think about throughout my day. I asked Yahweh to meet me where I was, nourish this aching heart of mine, and love me back as His own.

With my limited yet creative imagination, Christ and I started dating. The morning and evening hours were sacred hours with my Lord and me. In the mornings, the front porch was our gathering place. I would awake with my fruits, Bible, and hymnal. The tall-green bamboo and the small brown birds were part of our scenery. In the evenings, our planned or spontaneous rendezvous coincided with the sun's setting. With His hand in mine, we talked about my day, what I liked and didn't like, the things I laughed about, the people I met during my day, and the recurring discourse—the healing process that was taking place. Once my mind was not engaged with another, the telephone line of heaven was open with me on the VIP line. "Dear Jesus, I love you." "Heavenly Father, thank you for waking me up this morning." "Dear God, but these people trying to have me sin my soul, they need to chill with all these checks and balances." (*Laughing to self*)

There was a Sunday that we had lunch on the greens. The multi-colored blanket lay on the prickly grass. On top of it was my wholesome meal and dessert. Who could resist fresh steamed vegetables, melt-in-your-mouth provision, and well-seasoned legumes with roasted nuts as the cherry on top? The topography of the high, lush green mountain grandeur stood before us. Only my mind heard the confabulation of my Lord and me. I was blushing from this divinely intimate exchange. One morning, as I left my place of residence for my morning engagement, small lilac flowers cascaded at my feet to cushion my steps. I knew the God who created the wind instructed it to release these flowers from the branches because the woman He died for needed a fragrant coronation.

The coronation was ensued by a timely makeover. The Godhead thus inspired me to go shopping and add color and design to my wardrobe. I started visiting a local hairstylist once every two weeks. I became more involved in social activities. Christian counseling was part of the process. I also had a very dear friend who helped me through my withdrawal symptoms from her. I will always love him for that. He stuck by my side. He never condemned. He kept it real. He understood. He constantly reminded me that God does not abandon us when we fall. God runs to us. God rescues us! There was renewed vigor in mission work. Jesus and I had divine dates, all to rekindle the lost love. I was loved and growing in love as I experienced the ebb and flow of divine intimacy. The best part of this recurrent pattern was its impact on my self-intimacy; I believed in myself, loved me, and saw me. Once more, I was attractive. Now, my mattress became my place of rejuvenation, my pillow became the depository of my thanksgiving, and my sheet was the needed comfort at the end of my day. I was alive again.

I share this story for the benefit of three people. The first one is for *me*. Satan can no longer use that part of my forgiven history to cause me shame. The second person is *you/them*, a Christian who struggles with same-sex attraction or other sexual immorality. God will rescue you. God still loves you. The 3rd person is for *you too*. These are those whose description of homosexuality is the only abomination. When you do this, you nullify the value of Christ's spilled blood. Proverbs 6:16-19 "These six things doth the Lord hate: yea, seven are an abomination unto him: a proud look, a lying tongue, hands that shed innocent blood, that deviseth wicked imaginations, feet that be swift in running to mischief, a false witness that speaketh lies, and he that soweth discord among brethren."

Respectfully, if *you too* can't help those who struggle with same-sex attraction, I implore you to do what Jesus would do. If you have been a beneficiary of His grace, I leave that encounter to inspire that response. If you haven't experienced first-hand what grace does, I beseech you to rummage through the Gospels for that treasure. It is "ungodly" to condemn but "godly" to pray earnestly for any soul espoused by sin. Be kind, or else keep quiet if the Spirit doesn't inspire you to speak.

I thank God that He did not leave me in darkness but gave me a testimony of sexual and emotional healing. For the person reading whose thirsty soul has been quenched by my testimony, come to the well and see a man who has saved, forgiven, and redeemed me. He waited for me by my pit/well of sexual abuse, perversion, indiscretion, and illegitimacy to rescue and restore me to right living in and through Him. Come see and experience the redemptive power of my man, Christ Jesus!

Meet Shasta Green

Shasta Green was born on the nature island of the Caribbean, Dominica. She is a Christian and an eager traveler who relishes spending time in nature. She delights in meeting new people and is keen on portraying Christ.

She currently lives and works in Trinidad and Tobago as a counselor and occupational therapist. Her motto is: "Everything happens for a reason." Her treasured Bible text is Psalm 86:5, "For thou, Lord, art good, and ready to forgive; and plenteous in mercy unto all them that call upon thee."

Her favorite hymn is "Moment by Moment." Her prayer is that those who read her chapter will be encouraged and encourage others who feel shame for sexual sin to be lovingly reminded that God rescues, redeems, and restores. Shalom.

She can be reached at: micajegreen@gmail.com.

CHAPTER 5

Descending Deeper in the Pit

He brought me up also out of an horrible pit, out of the miry clay, and set my feet upon a rock, and established my goings. **(Psalms 40:2)**

Waiting has always been my greatest challenge in life. I was that person who walked with a hammer and a nail, trying to fix things in my own will and way. I usually get very anxious whenever I observe things not going how I want them to. Over time, God revealed that life doesn't work like that. He revealed the many things I lacked as a child of God, and two of them were patience and self-control.

Because I had many horrible experiences during childhood and adulthood, I resolved to take control of my life to protect myself. I became reserved and cautious about who I allowed in my life and dictated the terms by which they stayed. Although this seemed like a self-preservation mechanism, it was flawed because I did not always attract or allow the right people in my life and left no room for God's direction. Like an amateur builder, I erected a makeshift structure of my life until God stepped in and took over.

In the first book in the "Waiting in the Pit" trilogy, I related how God carried me through a dark time as I sang my way out of my pits. I did not mention that I was on an elevator, ascending and descending my life's pit. My Christian walk has been laced with highs and lows, progress and setbacks, learning and unlearning, committing to trust God, and doubting His providence. I kept wondering when I'd finally get out of this quandary. When would I finally get to disembark this elevator that kept taking me up and down in my pits?

It was not until I was washing the dishes in my apartment in Chicago that I heard the Holy Spirit saying, "You have to go deeper in the pit to get out because the way you went in is not how you will get out." *What was the meaning of this?* I wondered. Immediately I felt a hefty burden, and then the Holy Spirit continued, "It is going to be very difficult and challenging, but it is something you have to go through."

After a series of disappointments and heartaches, I returned to New York City (NYC) after leaving five years prior. Initially, I had moved to escape my past troubles and get a fresh start. I was convinced I would meet my husband and experience certain breakthroughs, having made this move, but after five years, these desires still needed to be met. After years of living in Chicago, I suddenly felt the need to move back to New York, mainly because I missed my family and had an emotional attachment there.

When I got a call regarding a job opportunity from my part-time employer, I was convinced that it was confirmation that I should return to New York. For me, this was ideal because of the emotional interest I had there, and I would be around my family. However, what I thought and what God had planned did not coincide.

The packing process started, and the time was winding down quickly. It was a bittersweet time because I gained a family while living in Chicago, and now, I was about to move away from them. After announcing my departure, my church family hosted an appreciation sendoff celebration in our honor. It was very emotional because I did not realize that my little family, consisting of myself, my daughter, and my niece, were valued to this extent by these people or that we had impacted them so notably.

When I got home that night, I cried for a long while. I then realized that all along, I thought the reason I was led to Chicago by the Lord was to meet my earthly husband, but instead, I had met my Heavenly Husband, my Kinsman Redeemer, who is none other than the Lord Jesus Christ. I had gotten incredibly close and experienced Him on a deeper and more intimate level there. I also gained a whole church family in the process. You see, even though I had given my life to Him over eleven years prior, I never took the time to get to know Him meaningfully. Coming to Chicago, I experienced His loving kindness through my many trials and learned to appreciate His presence and workings in my life.

When I arrived in New York, I discovered that the promised job was not yet ready. There was a delay with the project, and my boss could not assure me of a tentative or possible commencement

Descending Deeper in the Pit

date. I was informed that, in the interim, I would work in New Jersey until the project was launched. I started working in New Jersey and had to take six transportations daily, three in the morning and three in the evening, to get to and from work.

Each day while commuting, I observed a cluster of constructions underway at both train stations where I traversed: Penn Station, New York, and Elizabeth, New Jersey. Each site had a huge picture showing what the finished product would look like.

One day, after getting off the New Jersey Transit and heading to the office, the thought came to mind that the longer the construction process, the more prominent and enduring the outcome. God was telling me that even though I had been waiting on Him for what seemed to be a long time, He was doing something great within me. For that to happen, He must take the time to carefully build me from the foundation up because whatever He does will last forever. Even though there is no picture with a preview of the finished work, I am confident that whatever He is doing in and on me will be perfectly beautiful.

Consequently, I read an article regarding the construction process because I wanted a better

understanding, and something stood out. A part of the article said that "Every construction project, regardless of size, benefits from a solid and great project manager who is familiar with construction project management." We are all under construction, and the comforting reality is that we have the greatest Architect and Project Manager who is more than familiar and qualified with our construction process because He who created us has a plan and design for our lives. (Jeremiah 29:11) I then realized He was still working on my foundation, hence, my constant descent into the pit. The deeper the hole or pit, the sturdier and more secure the pillars that will hold up the building.

I've seen where I have gone deeper into the pit and felt God was about to reveal more to me. God showed me why I was constantly plunging into these pits because I spent years dwelling on past traumas, and even though I convinced myself that my past was not affecting me anymore, I was still battling, which created turmoil within.

For years, I used the hammer and nail I walked around with to chip holes and dents in the foundation God was laying for me. This meant my foundation needed to be more solid, and if the Project Manager wasn't convinced that the foundation of my life was adequately laid, He would not apply the frame and build out the structural framework.

I was always in survival mode exuding the "I can do it by myself" mentality. Being a single parent gets overwhelming, forcing me to be self-reliant and tough. This, along with past hurts and disappointment, steeled my psyche and left me feeling like I always had to be in control and needed no one. I did not realize I was also saying I didn't need God. This mentality developed impatience and anxiety. I was like the foolish man that built his house on the sand.

I prayed for many things over the years, and God finally revealed that I had been standing in my way all this time. My poor choices would interfere with the process whenever He cast the foundation that would lift me from my pits. I was always in fight or flight mode. I kept running ahead of God because I could not wait. I was also struggling with self-doubt and fear. These created inconsistency and procrastination in my life.

Looking back now, I've seen how being inconsistent led others to believe I was confused about my purpose. I have been in the rocking chair mode, going back and forth, with no progress. Whenever I got close to getting something good, I panicked because of the negative thoughts that consumed me, and then I took flight. In doing this, I pushed people away. I've learned over time that fear causes us to limit ourselves even when God is expanding the avenues in our lives. Self-doubt caused me to drift further from God because He said, "I have a plan for you, and it is to prosper you." I replied, "Time is running out, and if I don't do something about it, I will never get what I want." So, I started doing my own thing.

God had to bring me deeper into the pit because I had become chronically impatient, and patience is critical to strengthening our faith and growing us spiritually. *"...tribulation worketh patience; and patience, experience; and experience, hope "* (Romans 5:3-4). I tried to climb out of the pit, convincing myself that God was taking me out, but I fell flat on my face every time because I kept going back to the things, He was keeping me away from. I was "like a dog returning to its vomit" (Proverbs 26:11). I have been foolish because of my impatience and not having self-control. The Holy Spirit showed me that I had to be mindful of how much time I spent dwelling in the past and milking my emotions. God started to give me visions of how things could go if I did not allow Him to lead because He could see what I couldn't.

Unlike me, God had the full picture. He knew the dimensions, density, measurements, and materials needed to get me to where He was taking me. He brought me to Matthew 6:33 "But seek ye first the kingdom of God, and His righteousness; and all these things will be added to you." I did not adhere, so He allowed me to face the consequences of sitting in the dark pits I plunged into until I faced my demons. If I had sought Him before making my decisions, things would have been much better than they turned out to be.

When the Holy Spirit said I had to go deeper into the pits, I thought it meant returning to New York to live permanently. However, He took me back there for a short stint because it was critical to mending my foundation. He had to repair the breaches where the cracks and holes were and reconstruct His purpose for me. I was supposed to trust God and not lean on my understanding, but instead, I trusted what I saw and felt was the right thing to do. I constructed a plan. I would slide down in the pit most conveniently, stay at my mom's house for a little while, get settled in work, get an apartment, and figure my way. The promise of getting a promotion meant things would go well; it would all work out!

Months passed, and I heard nothing about the promotion, so more time was needed, and I resolved to wait. While waiting, it became apparent that God was beckoning to me. Finally, I started looking in His direction. I began to pray and spend more time with Him, and while spending time, He revealed to me that what

Descending Deeper in the Pit

I was pursuing was not His plan. *What do you mean? You made the way for me to come here. You said I had to go deeper in the pit to get out. I don't understand.*

I failed to see that I had run ahead of God. I was not moving in His timing or yielding to His leadership. Imagine making so many plans and then watching all of them crashing. I wasn't paid what was promised, so I worked for a salary that could only cover bills and transportation. I continued working while I searched for another job but was unsuccessful.

Deep down, I was still holding on to the empty promotion promises. I could not afford an apartment because I was not compensated enough, so I had to stay a little longer at my mom's house, which was a great inconvenience. God did not allow anything to go as I planned because He had a better plan.

God led me in a season of revelation, repentance, and restoration. He showed me His intentions while He slowly impressed on my heart that I had returned to New York to recalibrate and fix the breaches in the foundation. I needed to make peace with my past, resolve many issues, close many chapters left open in New York, and then move on.

I wrestled with God for a while because I felt I was plummeting into an endless pit with no hope of getting out. I started to worry about what others would think about me packing up everything and coming to New York, then having to return to Chicago in a matter of months. I started thinking about how confused I would appear but allowed the process to take its course.

Waiting In the Pit

I resigned from my job and prayerfully sought God's leading on how to proceed. God saw that even though I was doing my best to follow Him, I was still struggling, so He inspired my friends to pray with me and strengthen me with the Word. I then went back to Him for more guidance and prayed that if it's His will for me to go back to Chicago, He should align everything. Immediately after saying this prayer, the pit's elevator lit, indicating I would start my ascent. Gradually and miraculously, things began to fall into place. Imagine I left a vast apartment in Chicago and came to New York, sleeping on my mother's couch in a small house in NY. I walked away from an excellent job within walking distance from my apartment to traveling almost two hours one way to work every day.

I left from being treated with dignity and respect by my previous employers to being demeaned and manipulated by my employer in New Jersey. Even though the girls were excited to be closer to family, they were very sad shortly after landing in NY because they no longer had their own space and resented the school they were attending. I went from attending church and ministering frequently to staying in bed on Sabbaths. This was never God's intention for me, but He still worked things out on my behalf.

I gave God complete control, and He orchestrated and operated all the machinery necessary to take me out of the pit. The deeper I got into Him, the more I could feel Him elevating me. The transition back to Chicago was mind-blowingly smooth. Debts I had incurred were miraculously paid before I returned. I was reinstated in my old job and assigned to a better department with a higher salary than before I left Chicago. Yes, I got a promotion!

The girls transitioned smoothly back to their old school. Our Chicago church family embraced us lovingly as the father with the prodigal son, assisting us to settle and committing to supporting us in every way possible. God restored us!

I needed to close doors in NY and make peace with past traumas. My relationship with my family was good before returning, but it improved after spending a few months with them. When I initially left New York in 2018, I ran, not from anyone but from myself. Running was my way of dealing with my issues, and because I was going through an emotionally dark time, I decided to escape. God took me deeper into the pit to anchor my faith in Him, to help me release the burdens I was carrying, and to appreciate His direction in my life. While in this very long waiting season, I learned that if my foundation is not on Christ Jesus, He cannot erect the structure He designed for my life.

God is rewriting my story right now. The former book is closed, and the new one has opened. I am allowing God to write this story because I had made a mess of my story in the past. Now, I am relying on Him entirely. I will not move unless He says I should, and as He writes each line, I will walk, and when He decides to pause, I will wait, even if I am to build a tent until He starts writing again; then I will move. I have done enough and have been standing in my way for far too long.

God took me deeper into my pit to face my anxieties, trauma, depression, self-condemnation, self-doubt, self-pity, procrastination, and inconsistency! Now that I am more self-aware, I am elevating as I allow Him to heal me and make my life a masterpiece.

Meet Serena Rowe

Serena Rowe is a Jamaican native residing in the USA. God has endowed her with numerous gifts. She is a recording artist who ministers in song and a songwriter. She is also co-author of *Waiting in the Pit I*. God has blessed her with an eye for creativity; thus, she is also a graphic/website designer and a video editor.

Serena makes herself available to do her part in spreading the gospel wherever the Lord leads. Presently, Serena ministers at several churches upon request.

Serena volunteers at various organizations and continues to give of herself to help make a difference. She was recognized by the Municipal Council of The City of Paterson, New Jersey, for Community Service and Women's Right Advocacy.

www.serenaroweministries.org

Instagram: Seri songbird

YouTube: Serena Rowe Ministries

CHAPTER 6

Pit of Grace

"And we know that all things work together for good to those who love God, to those who are called according to His purpose." **(Romans 8:28)**

As we hustled to feed Whiskey, our hungry fluffy black and white Poodle/Scottish Terrier, I contemplated the exciting trip we were about to embark on to the University of the Southern Caribbean at Maracas Valley. I also mused about our tightly held plans for a dramatic musical play; all tossed together on that eventful one-off public holiday!

That holiday on October 10th, 2006, in my homeland of Trinidad and Tobago, was earmarked to honor the Chinese contribution to our Rainbow Nation and heralded the beginning of unimaginable changes in our family's life. In the dialectic words of an old Proverb, "What eh meet yuh eh pass yuh!" (What you haven't gone through yet, don't believe it can't happen) You'll understand as I unravel.

Waiting In the Pit

Married then for twenty years, mother of a twelve-year-old son, a banker by profession, and fully entwined in youth ministry in my church, I felt fulfilled and blessed. I remember being excited and consumed with the musical play I had been writing. It was my first ever musical as a playwright! I wrote the lyrics, recorded the tunes in my head, and planned to visit a musician friend at the University of the Southern Caribbean to request his expertise in writing the musical score sheets for my songs. Talk about a tall order? Yes, it certainly was! A tall order spilling over with dramatic excitement!

Now, packed for an interesting day, my husband organized food for this pup, a gift our son begged and pleaded for, promising to be a *faithful* pet owner. Was he faithful? Not at all! I will never forget the image of my husband, frozen in a bend-over position, dog bowl in hand, and the sound of his loud moan of pain. A painful moan that I had never heard escaped from this man who never complained of feeling sick and operated as though he was always charged with Duracell batteries. He could barely whisper. With gritted teeth and excruciating back pain, he could not straighten his body. Even with our help, tears welled in his eyes as he gingerly sat on the garage step. My rapid fearful inquiries aggravated the situation because, with all the shocking pain he was experiencing, he insisted on still making the trip, perhaps not to disappoint me.

Looking back now, I realize there is a blur. We had the initial meeting about the music, but the play never materialized. On our way home, he handed over the steering wheel to his cousin, who would have been the pianist for the project. This truly confirmed something was seriously wrong, as there was no way he would have done so otherwise.

The days following were strange. It was as though I was viewing our lives in a slow, scary-motion film. Doctor's visits, x-rays, painkillers, platelets dropping, and no definite diagnosis. I was balancing going to work, taking time off to be a supportive wife and comforting nurse, and being in a daze: more unanswered questions, prayers, and tears. Doubled over or even getting down on all his fours at times, my husband suffered through excruciating pain. Blood tests were done, but still no conclusive word from the doctors. The upheaval of our lives chiseled away at my faith.

After weeks of wondering why God had inflicted our small closely-knit family with this uncertain infirmity, I felt stripped of my usual unassuming strength. Was it punishment for wrongs done? I secretly questioned myself. "Lord! Please, Lord! I dare not attempt an answer!" Publicly, I was still exhibiting a brave face of resolve but mentally crumbling! I could observe my son silently processing the drastic change in our lives, where Daddy was unable to be Daddy anymore, and Mummy was being strangely cool and struggling to be normal. Unsuccessfully so! The telltale signs around my eyes belied my efforts. After weeks of these complications, my younger brother suggested that we see a top doctor specializing in Hematology, who, fortunately, was his childhood friend and school colleague. Oh yes! We knew him as he was originally from our village in South Trinidad. He was booked up for months, but upon hearing of the situation, he squeezed us in for a visit.

Waiting In the Pit

The trip to Port of Spain took twice the time, as our family friend had driven or, should I say, crawled 30 mph so Walter would not be in so much pain. Looking at the x-ray and listening intently to the symptoms, Dr. Charles knew exactly what was wrong but waited to share it with us then. He urgently advised that my husband be hospitalized in Port of Spain General Hospital for further blood work, where he would be his patient. It seemed like everything was moving at a snail's pace until it all culminated with the diagnosis—multiple myeloma! What's that? We had never heard those two words before. The doctor spoke to Walter. Initially, he thought it didn't sound too serious, but he was speechless and mortified when Dr. Charles explained it. My husband asked Dr. Charles to explain it to me as he was very emotional and didn't know how I would take the shattering news!

Multiple Myeloma is a cancer of plasma cells. Plasma cells are a type of white blood cell in the bone marrow. The x-ray showed one of his vertebrae collapsed due to the debilitating disease. I was told it was very aggressive, and Walter had between six months and a stretch to live one year! What!?

What is he saying!? I fought back the tears. "Is there no treatment for this?" I asked defiantly. Dr. Charles patiently explained that a bone marrow transplant could be done abroad, costing over a million dollars. That was the only treatment known, offering a life extension of approximately three years. Walter was looking at me helplessly, tearfully, and hopelessly. We were traumatized by this devastating news! I felt like my heart had stopped, but I remember telling Dr. Charles that God would make a way. Somehow, this was the appropriate thing to say, with all the correct learned

Christian cliches I knew to say. Really? What did I know about this type of abject adversity?

The doctor was shaking his head in agreement, a questioning agreement, if only to give needed comfort at that time. I knew at that moment Dr. Charles was doing his best to make my husband as comfortable as he could, sourcing bags of precious blood that Walter needed urgently.

My husband was fragile and looked completely defeated. So, although I felt as if all my internal organs were shivering or was it the cold temperature of the Port of Spain General Hospital, I screamed and bawled without a sound escaping my lips. I had to be strong. My head was reeling with questions I could not ask and thoughts I dared not verbalize. Is it so easy for disaster to step in? Why was God allowing this to happen to us? Weren't we serving Him faithfully? What should I do? I needed to get a grip on myself as I felt that my head would burst open!

First and foremost, how do I deliver this news to our son, our relatives, friends, and church family? I dreaded the questions, the pity! The well-intentioned words of empathy. I didn't want to hear any of it. I just wanted to blink and have this nightmarish moment in time disappear.

Disappear, please!

I felt like I was falling deeper and deeper into a dark bottomless pit, where I was trying desperately to find my footing on familiar terrain. Still, alas, familiarity was something of the past, for life as I knew it would never be the same again. All my mental and emotional struggles were masked to face the world: to accept any help necessary, to heroically organize fundraisers, to embrace my son and assure him that I'll do my best—my motherly best!

I was concerned about how this traumatic jolt in our lives would affect him psychologically. How would he flourish and develop as a young man without his father? This is crazy, Lord! Never in my deepest thoughts of family life did I expect this. In our church lives, we functioned in various capacities. My husband was an elder who preached about adversity, about Job's experience in the Bible. We also served as family life coordinators, discussing family crises and the like; now, it was at our doorsteps. It was time to put what we read and counseled about into our lives in a practical way. It was time to depend wholly upon the Jesus we spoke so much about. *Lord, Lord, help us!* I felt unprepared!

After weeks of hospitalization, of getting phone calls from Walter some nights relating hallucinated stories of people flying through the window trying to get him, of fights with the nurses as they tried to restrain him from attempts to get out of bed, of understanding the side effects of the powerful drug being administered to him, he was discharged. Wheelchair-bound, grateful to be in familiar surroundings and to thank God for life, he cried shamelessly, emotionally hugging our son. He said he didn't think he would leave the hospital alive. We all hugged and cried. It was sad, but it felt good to cry out! There were changes to the flow of our home for the necessary care to be administered. The kindness and benevolence of our friends was overwhelming! God provided everything we needed to have him as comfortable as possible. Everything!

I'll never forget a dear friend whose kindness provided an adjustable power bed, wheelchair, walker, bed pans, etc. God showed me I was not alone, even in my pit of hopelessness. He was assuring me that He wouldn't leave me. He wouldn't forsake us in our time of desperation.

Grappling with the way forward, I decided we would seek the services of a naturopathic doctor we heard about. He was of German origin, a medical doctor who used natural and holistic remedies. He was disenchanted with the politics of big pharmaceutical policies. He recounted that he had written the international powers-that-be with researched procedural steps and tried medicinal cures for cancer, but he was shut down. We were guided to this stern, no-nonsense doctor for help.

We traveled to East Trinidad with hope in our hearts; hope we got; yes, hope with an understanding of the discipline needed, the changes in diet, and the preparation of food. Hearing those words, "All is not lost," from the lips of Dr. Dorch was reassuring. He was thorough as he reviewed and explained Walter's clinical reports and the effects of multiple myeloma on the human body.

We left with varied herbal supplements, a recipe for a special tonic to build immunity and tone the body, guidelines for food preparation, and a list of food items to remove from our kitchen pantry and refrigerator. Wow! It was a lot, but as the little servant girl in the biblical story of Captain Naaman, I quickly encouraged my husband that it was worth trying. We had nothing to lose. He could have no processed foods, tin stuff, meats, dairy products, sugar, table salt, etc. "The body needed to be alkaline to regenerate new cells;" Dr. Dorch's words stayed with me.

I knew I had to be the driving force to follow and stick to the diet plan, so we employed a family member as the day nurse, and my shift began around 6:00 pm during the work week.

Tough? Yes, but it had to be done. The extension and quality of life depended on it. I would come home from work and head to his bed to hear about his day. Most times, I would see the frustration in his eyes, and that caused my heart to sink. My son didn't talk much. I had to pry out his thoughts and feelings from day to day.

Nevertheless, I felt God's hand guiding us. The support and love of our church family at Siparia SDA Church, the consistent fervent prayers on behalf of our family, and the prayer warriors worldwide were felt. I experienced daily strength to push on. Looking back, even though I could not handle the safety of the solid ground, my pit experience was now one of buoyancy. I was no longer tumbling in dark despair but being kept afloat and being urged by the Holy Spirit that our only help comes from God!

As the months went by, I could see improvements in Walter's overall well-being. The diet plan, herbal tonic, and God's answer to contrite prayers began that good work. We discussed raising funds with the bone marrow transplant in view! Over one million Trinidad and Tobago dollars! It was a tall order, but I had to try, and we did.

Letters requesting public and corporate donations deposited to a specific account for public scrutiny, a Gospel concert, a boat cruise, a food-tasting event organized by our family friend, various church contributions from many different denominations, and a special grant to assist Government employees made it all possible. It was heartwarming to see the benevolent responses and tangible feedback we received. God be praised! The biggest miracle, though, was my health insurance coverage. After doubting that I should even try, and consistently haggling with the management of the company for weeks, God just opened a way where there seemed to be no way. Glory to God! As one of my all-time favorite songs by Larnelle Harris says, "He made a road in the wilderness, as only He can do; He made a road in the wilderness, and the power of love grow through."

Only God can turn Pharaoh-like NOs into unwilling Yesses! Furthermore, the delayed period allowed an enhanced package to be approved! This was miraculous, phenomenal, and groundbreaking, as insurance coverage was our company's first of its kind. Years later, colleagues from other branches called me for advice as they heard about my experience. My pit experience at this time is aptly described in Psalms 91:2, "I will say of the Lord, He is my refuge and my fortress: my God; in Him will I trust." So, with the contributed funds and donations, the maximum insurance payout we could have received and hospital discounts for the bone marrow transplant became possible! What a mighty God we serve!

What appeared to be sure pronounced death, falling into the pit of utter despair, darkness, and anguish at the sentence of my dear husband and life partner, was a difficult yet miraculously, unforgettable account of God's love! That pit of despair testified to others that God would not leave us alone in adversity. Due to my loving sister's choicest intervention, the bone marrow transplant was done successfully at Addenbrookes Hospital in Cambridge, England. Instead of three (3) years of life extension, Walter received six (6) precious years of remission from that dreaded disease. That totaled seven (7) years from diagnosis! In this precious time, he saw our son off to university. This amazing God that we serve prepared and cushioned us to grieve and be comforted. Walter's years of remission were God's mercy and compassion poured out to grant us a less complicated landing.

Many who witnessed God's benevolence in our pit of sickness and grief, including family, friends, and church family, were impacted, comforted, and blessed. As if from heavenly harps, the comforting music to these words was played: "When you pass through the waters, I will be with you, and through the rivers, they shall not overflow you. When you walk through the fire, you shall not be burned, nor shall the flames scorch you." Isaiah 43:2 What an awesome promise! This was manifested and proclaimed as a witness to all! Indescribable! Yes, indescribable is our God! Walter sleeps in Jesus, and we look forward to that great getting up morning! What a day that will be!

This pit experience is a powerful reminder that our loving Heavenly Father can use what was meant for our destruction and utter ruin, to shelter us through stormy times. Whatever pit you may be waiting in, I pray you will experience His grace, love, and mercy, because He is in the fire with you, defeating the enemy and working out your victorious deliverance!

Meet Joy Pilgrim-Briggs

Joy Pilgrim-Briggs is a native of Trinidad & Tobago currently residing in Florida, USA. She is married to Michael Briggs and mothers an adult son. She is a retired banker who spent thirty-eight years in the banking industry as a qualified certified financial advisor. She is a devout Christian who has spent over decades in church leadership and served in most church departments, including youth leadership, family life, Sabbath school, personal ministries, women's ministries, church clerk.

She is passionate about drama ministry, where she has written and directed over ten plays. One of her most significant accomplishments in this department is spearheading a two-weeks drama crusade, which was the first of its kind at the South Caribbean Conference TT. She has also served as president of (UFCHM) South Caribbean Conference chapter.

Her hobbies include singing, drama, traveling, hiking, scrabbling, and cooking. Her favorite Scripture is John 3:17: For God sent not His Son into the world to condemn the world, but that the world through Him might be saved.

CHAPTER 7

Stacked Coal Pit

"The Lord is nigh unto all them that call upon him, to all that call upon him in truth. He will fulfil the desire of them that fear him: he also will hear their cry and will save them." **(Psalms 145:18-19)**

"A**NGELIC**"
"What? Angelique? Angela? Angelia? Angel?"
"No. Okay, just call me Angie."

Oh, how I detested my name. Why Angelic? Where did my parents discover that name? Why not Alicia or Maria? I really loved Maria. I often pondered, *is it because of my name that I am a constant target to the enemy? Is this why I have been in so many pits all my life?*

My name was loathsome. I despised it except at Christmas when I heard it mentioned in "Hark the Herald Angels Sing." I couldn't wait to become an adult to change it. Now, knowing its meaning (like an angel; messenger of God), I have accepted my name. I have embraced the notion that I AM A MESSENGER, as God has given me many chronicles to fuel the lives of others.

I AM LIVING A FIFTH LIFE after surviving seven major surgeries. Come journey with me as I share the many experiences where I felt stacked, burnt, and buried like a coal pit. Each encounter could have ended my life. Instead, they are my testimonies that have glorified God and fueled and blessed others.

Pit #1 - I remember that evening vividly. My husband, Calvin, of two years, and I were leaving the church compound after the church service when I received the death news of a friend. I wasn't aware that he was ill. The cause of his death was disturbing. He died of acquired immunodeficiency syndrome (AIDS). A flurry of thoughts and questions swirled in my mind. He was single, a Christian, a brilliant teacher, and a church member. AIDS? How? I don't understand. This was very surprising, even more baffling. As we left the compound, I remember telling Calvin, "I am so upset; I don't want to drive," so I hurried into the passenger seat and closed the door. Calvin responded, "Okay."

We proceeded away from the church and the area where we resided en route to collect my aunt and uncle, who were vacationing from England. Midway along the ride, we were near an unlit forested area familiar to us. The moisture on the road was evidence of a moderate drizzle of rain. I had a careless habit of sitting with my legs extended on the dashboard. This was easy and comfortable as our vehicle was outfitted with a seatbelt only for the driver. I felt uneasy.

"Calvin, could you slow down?" I asked.

"I am not driving fast!"

"I know, but slow down, please."

He obeyed.

"Did we pray before leaving the church?"

"I didn't pray and can't remember you praying."

"Yes, I prayed."

To appropriate a posture for prayer, I removed my legs from the dashboard, adjusted my seat uprightly, and commenced praying. All I recall saying was, "Lord, help us. Lord, have mercy on us!"

Suddenly, I saw long legs bolting out of the bushes.

"WHAT IS THAT?"

It was a large black cow! There was also a car heading in the opposite direction. The cow ran so swiftly that I was bewildered. After the deafening crash, the impact of my head on the windscreen became obvious. Calvin did not turn in the vehicle's direction, which was filled with six people. The large cow hurled into the air landed on the hood and settled in front of the vehicle. For months I could see the bulging eyes of the animal rolling down the windscreen whenever I closed my eyes to sleep.

On top of that, when our vehicle finally came to a stop, another vehicle struck us from behind, pushing our vehicle over the cow. After violently convulsing, sadly, the animal died. How I got onto the road, in the large crowd, bare feet, screaming and stamping in the splinters, I can't recollect. I hardly remember what happened

Stacked Coal Pit

next, except I was in the general hospital, San Fernando, in excruciating pain with a cervical collar around my neck.

With the vehicle a total wreck, every physician voiced, "You are so lucky to be alive and didn't break your neck."

Calvin, "Girl, I snatched you from going through the windshield."

"Really? Really? Thank you."

Exodus 23:20 says, **"Behold, I send an Angel before thee, to keep thee in the way."** I know God spared my life that night. I struggled in a pit of pain and discomfort for the following year, my final year as a student nurse. In pain and tears, wearing a firm uncomfortable collar, I wrote and succeeded at my final examinations, as I refused to be referred for the following year. My reassurance came from **Philippians 4:13 "I can do all things through Christ which strengtheneth me."** That accident resulted in me enduring two lumbar laminectomies with internal fixations and reconstruction of my right shoulder. But…I WAS ALIVE!!

Pit #2 - Matriculation to commence my master's degree was October 1st of that year, the same month my annual medical was usually scheduled. Thrilled and optimistic, I started the program; however, during the Christmas holidays, I told my husband and children, "I don't feel myself, and both feet are swelling."

"Are you going to the doctor?"

"I will think about it, maybe after Christmas."

Waiting In the Pit

As a full-time employee, wife, and mother, I resolved *maybe it is due to fatigue and the extended sitting to complete my assignments.* After the excitement of ushering in the new year, I sought medical advice for my symptoms. The young Jamaican physician examined me.

"I'm sending you for further investigations on your legs and abdomen."

I said, "My annual medical last October was normal."

"That's fine," and he continued to script the orders.

A Doppler ultrasound was completed on both legs first. This was followed by an abdominal ultrasound scan (USS), sometimes called a sonogram. The findings piqued the interest of the technician. Her facial expression, which concerned me, soon turned to anxiety, worry, and fear as she was joined by two other colleagues, one of them her supervisor. After asking me the same questions in three different ways, he recommended an urgent MRI of my abdomen.

The USS was conducted on the same Friday I was due to travel to Miami to set sail on our wedding anniversary cruise. I considered postponing the trip as the fear of the unknown gripped me like a vice. With much coaxing and encouragement from my physician and family, I embarked on this long planned and awaited celebration. My husband, daughters, and I thoroughly enjoyed the experience; however, the thought of my possible diagnosis plagued my mind.

A Magnetic Resonance Imaging (MRI) was conducted immediately upon my return home. Waiting to receive the MRI results was arduous. After the interpretation, my gynecologist said, "I want you to see another colleague in Port of Spain; he has an additional specialty." After a brief phone conversation, the appointment was confirmed. An early morning trip the next day was needed to see this practitioner, who tried to be kind while breaking potentially bad news. This was Wednesday. I cannot forget his words, "I am 75% sure of the diagnosis; this can only be confirmed post-surgery; you need this procedure as of yesterday." Guilt and regret dominated my thoughts about going on my vacation.

I asked, "Did I neglect my health? Did I make a good decision? Was I irresponsible? Did I make a poor choice?"

Looking sad and worried, no one answered.

Friday of that same week, a five-hour surgery commenced my first treatment phase. I had never experienced such acute agonizing pain. After so many surgical procedures, I thought I knew what pain was; however, this pain pit was different. No analgesia seemed to be adequate or effective. Clothing seemed to contribute to the pain, so one night, I remember crying out to God in my nakedness. "Lord, I cannot take this pain anymore!" The heat and pressure in this pit were too much. After that night, my pain started to subside.

This was only the introduction to this layer in my pit, as ten days later, at my follow-up visit and removal of sutures, I received the news that I was dreading. I was diagnosed with a life-threatening critical illness, which interrupted all my plans for the following year, including my studies. Everything except my treatment had to be placed on a back burner. This pit was pressing and burning everything in me. The side effects of the treatment were unpleasant and sometimes unbearable. During this time, **3 John 2, "Beloved, I wish above all things that thou mayest prosper and be in health, even as thy soul prospereth,"** was the promise that reminded me of God's wish for my soul and my health.

Thankfully, much later than anticipated, without any additional cost, I travelled to Canterbury, England, with my daughters to walk the stage to collect my certificate after the master's program. The intimate details of this uncomfortable coal pit have encouraged so many women. I continue to share my story anonymously as I await God's timing to share openly.

Pit - #3 Have you ever received help from the most unforeseen source? **Philippians 4:19, "But my God shall supply all your need according to his riches in glory by Christ Jesus,"** became very personal to me.

"I'm so excited I could hardly sleep last night like my imagination was in overdrive."

Calvin, "I slept like a baby."

"Boy, I can't wait to see the places I read about as a child."

I consider myself a seasoned traveler; however, it was my first time there. We arrived at Indira Gandhi International in New Delhi after a twelve-hour flight, initially scheduled for ten. Due to a dispute between Pakistan and India, permission was denied for flying over their air space. We heard that we flew over Iran and

Afghanistan; this was hair-raising. We connected in Pune, North India, where we met Dr. Sinclair, who took us to the hotel.

Our warm welcome included flower garlands around our necks and a large bouquet of fresh flowers for me. I felt special as the staff greeted us in the foyer. It was Friday. We were exhausted, so we rested for much of the Sabbath. The large hotel was beautiful, clean, and aligned with international standards. North Indian delicacies were attractively displayed, delicious, different, and spicy; however, other choices, like South Indian, Japanese, Asian and continental, were also available.

"I've never seen mangos used to make so many desserts."

"Look!! Tarts and cheesecake too."

I particularly enjoyed Mumbai Bunda, Chole Kulche, Sambar, and Dalia Upma. The use of surplus food at the hotel haunted me, as evidence of hunger and poverty witnessed outside the hotel was unimaginable.

I implored, "What happens to the excess food?"

"It is dumped."

"What? Dumped?" I was flabbergasted as I learned it was against the hotel's policy to distribute to the impoverished. Wow! This was overwhelming. I had to make a deliberate effort to cope with the gloomy sights of dejection. Bagging food for distribution on the streets afforded me a minuscule level of temporary consolation as I was continually reminded that this was their reality.

We did some exploration; Sahar Road shopping, the market, malls, Mumbai, Maharashtra, the Gateway to India, and the Taj Mahal Hotel are just a few places we saw. My highlights were the Golden Temple and the Taj Mahal. We also visited the Ellora Caves, a UNESCO World Heritage Site. This historic temple proved to be fascinating. Temperatures that day soared to 43 degrees C or 109 degrees F. I didn't feel well by evening but was determined to enjoy my trip.

The following day, I felt worse. We were invited to visit an Indian family, friends of our host. My husband asked if I was sure I wanted to go to lunch. I kept my commitment. I was delighted to be inside a typical home, to understand how families lived, and to experience their customs and practices. Women served their guests, men, children, then themselves, in that order, and ate in separate rooms. Sitting on floor mats, we enjoyed an authentic Indian meal. Parting gifts were given to each of us. Mine was a beautiful orange sari.

By evening, I was having mild abdominal cramps. I couldn't understand why. I didn't eat street food, drink unbottled liquids, or use ice; everybody else was okay. The abdominal cramps intensified and were accompanied by vomiting and diarrhea. I self-medicated to the best of my ability, but the symptoms persisted.

After a sleepless night, Sunday morning I was fatigued, in pain, and dehydrated. Another member of our travel group welcomed two guests, members of her Hari Krishna Hindu group, to our hotel suite. They assembled in the living area to interact and worship. We occupied one of the bedrooms and could hear them in the distance.

I asked Calvin to request a doctor from the front desk. The hotel physician examined me and prescribed medication. I knew I was dehydrated and would benefit from intravenous (IV) support. "Doc, do you think I need IV Fluids?" I asked.

"You should be fine with the prescription."

I voiced my disagreement. "I think I do."

I felt disgusted; he did not consider my suggestion. The medications taken were ineffective.

The guests were departing, so we were invited to meet them. I quickly declined. I felt and looked so horrible; I couldn't meet anyone like that. I was still in bed, in sleepwear, and had no energy to get dressed. Next came a knock on the door. Two medium-built young devotees entered our room, dressed in cotton Dhoti and wearing Kanthi-mala (neck beads). I tried to smile as we introduced ourselves. They were fluent in English, so we exchanged pleasantries and small conversations regarding our trip.

The shorter one spoke, "I heard about your ordeal last night. I am a qualified medical doctor," Can I examine your hands, with your permission, of course?" My symptoms had still not improved, so I agreed. Hesitantly, I allowed him to examine my hands. He said, "You need IV fluids immediately." Before I could answer, he left and returned shortly with a bag of IV fluid, an IV line, an angiocath, and other medication. He was so gentle, polite, and reassuring, and he refused to accept the funds we offered. After

Waiting In the Pit

several unsuccessful attempts, he said, "You need to go to the hospital."

That was the last thing I wanted to hear. "Hospital? In India? On my vacation? No way!" I protested. It took some time to convince me. I felt so weak; after a while, I just went along. Vaguely, I remember him calling someone on his cell phone, conversing in his native dialect, and being placed in the vehicle. What happened next was a big blur. I was so lethargic. I was uncertain where I was and why so many people were around. Why was I in a wheelchair? Where was I? Calvin later explained all the details.

I spent five (5) days in Noble Hospital, Hadapsar, Pune. Calvin was given a bed. The initial challenge was to commence the IV, which proved complicated as many of my superficial blood vessels had collapsed and were inaccessible. Discussions regarding a venous cut-down were held. This is an emergency procedure where the vein is surgically exposed, and a cannula is inserted under direct vision when peripheral cannulation is difficult or impossible. With the assistance of infrared light and a pediatric cannula, clotted blood was aspirated, and an IV was commenced. I was oblivious to what was happening.

Another IV line was inserted. My symptoms continued, leading to a decreased appetite and weight loss. Investigations included physical examinations, vital signs monitoring, blood, and ultra-sonography. The spotless surroundings and knowledgeable, kind, and caring staff contributed to my recovery. My medication regime was timely; I received visits from physicians, nurses, nurse managers, dieticians, and customer service representatives. I expressed my thanks in gratitude to the two Hindu devotees and

Stacked Coal Pit

looked forward to their daily visits. Subsequently, I learned that the physician cancelled his flight to ensure I received the best care. What a blessing!!

After over SIXTY bouts of diarrhea, my symptoms subsided. At discharge, I saw the outside of the hospital for the first time as I reminisced on **Isaiah 65:24, "And it shall come to pass, that before they call, I will answer; and while they are yet speaking, I will hear."** Like Daniel, God showed me favor in a strange land.

Before I got ill, help was already on the way. The physician flew for three hours and drove for over an hour to get to the hotel, and his colleague travelled by train for three days. I felt honored and humbled by this intervention, as the climax of this pit could have been tragic. God provided just what I needed–an English-speaking physician with all the necessary connections. I am forever grateful to these two Hindu devotees. What an awesome God we serve!!

Pit #4 - It was the day before my dad's ninetieth birthday celebration, so I was busy packing to drive to his home. I planned to spend the night, sing happy birthday early in the morning and continue the preparation. I didn't observe that the air-conditioning unit was dripping behind the curtain, causing a puddle of water on the floor. Suddenly, I found myself slowly slipping on my tiled bedroom floor. My right leg stretched to the front of me while my left leg skated to the back. I could not stop or support myself and felt a tearing sensation behind my upper right leg. I continued to a complete split on the floor.

"CALVIN! CALVIN! CAL, CAL!!"

Unfortunately, my husband didn't hear the loud shrieking scream as the door was closed. I couldn't move; I was in so much pain and tears. The telephone was out of my reach, so I remained in this position. After what seemed like an eternity, my husband entered the room. "What happened? WHY ARE YOU ON THE FLOOR? WHY DIDN'T YOU CALL ME!?" In shock, he hastened to assist me to my feet. There was a huge, dark swelling the size of a grapefruit at the back of my leg.

"OH LAWD, this is so painful; I can't press on this foot."

After icing and analgesia, we visited a physician. Investigations confirmed that I had torn my right hamstring muscle. "Lord!!" I said, "Another injury again? Another medical problem?" By now, I felt so fed up and frustrated with medical appointments, doctor's visits, hospitalizations, and surgeries. Little did I know that this was only the smoke! The fire was on its way. I wore a full-leg back-slab cast for eight weeks. This was my second cast as I sustained a left ankle fracture as a teenager.

As I tolerated this uncomfortable situation without the ability to shower or drive, three weeks later, I was interrupted one evening by an unexpected, sharp, sudden, ripping pain in my chest. I didn't know what was happening, but I knew something was wrong. Fortunately, my second daughter, Kalisha, was with me. "Take me to St. James now; call Khea and tell her what happened." She quickly took me to St. James Medical Facility, where I was treated. The doctor referred me to Port-of-Spain General for further management, against my wishes, as I would have preferred to be sent home and be treated by my private doctor. I prayed, Lord, you said in **Psalms 50:15, "And call upon me in the day of trouble: I will deliver thee, and thou shalt glorify me."**

After many hours of waiting in suspense, I was admitted, and a CT scan confirmed my diagnosis of bilateral pulmonary emboli. This life-threatening condition has caused the demise of countless others. I learned that the musculoskeletal injury in my leg was the precursor to this complication. Praise God, my life was spared again. Later, I returned to St. James to thank the physician for insisting that I be transferred. This saved my life. I was so thankful!!

As I write about this pit, I occasionally experience pain in my leg. I am still on medication and am being monitored. God has kept me through the stacking, burning, and pressing in my coal pit. I know He has me here for a purpose, and I submit to him to continue to use me as his messenger and the fuel that electrifies the lives of others. I continue to praise and thank him, and like David, I await His delivery time from this pressing coal pit. I will declare: **Psalms 40:2, "He brought me up also out of a horrible pit, out of the miry clay, and set my feet upon a rock, and established my goings."**

Meet Angelic Lezama-Clement

Angelic Lezama-Clement hails from the Republic of Trinidad and Tobago. She is a counselling psychologist and family life coach. She holds a Master of Arts in Counselling and Psychology–Warborough College (Ireland), and a Diploma in Clinical and Pastoral Counselling–Institute of Counselling (Scotland). She is also a registered nurse and a licensed midwife.

Married for the past thirty-seven years, she is a devoted wife and mother of two adult daughters and a granddaughter. She has served the church in Sabbath school, children's ministry, health, welfare, family life, and women's ministry. She is an avid reader who enjoys singing, listening to music, scrabbling, gardening, and travelling.

Angelic is passionate about teaching parenting skills, motivating families, and empowering young people to succeed. She founded Exclusive Counselling and Life Coaching Services and can be contacted at: exclusivecounsellingcoaching@gmail.com.

CHAPTER 8

Purpose In My Pit

"Transformation is a process, and as life happens there are tons of ups and downs. It's a journey of discovery - there are moments on mountaintops and moments in deep valleys of despair." – Rick Warren

The month of May, year, 2016 was a defining moment in my life. For the first time, I was fired from a job. I felt like my life could not have gotten worse than my prior experiences. Questions that had long been buried in the depths of my consciousness swiftly resurfaced as though they were just waiting in the shadows for the first opportunity to pounce.

Would I plunge deep into the dark pit of poverty once more? If so, was it even possible to permanently escape that dark place? Until now, I had worked tirelessly since the second decade of my life, fighting against all odds, climbing my way out of the pit on the ladder of education, rung by rung. And now, in one fell swoop, I found myself reliving those unfortunate experiences of my younger years at the bottom of this murky pit. The worst part was that there appeared to be no mode of escape in sight. As you might guess, I was utterly devastated, hopeless, and helpless.

Imagine being away from your family and suddenly being told you no longer had a job! Losing my job did not mean my obligations suddenly ceased—quite the contrary. I still had to contend with being alone in a new country with bills to pay and no quick solution in view.

As we often do when we become destitute, I questioned God. "*Why me?*" It is interesting how self-centered we become when we experience dire circumstances. We tend to believe that it's all about us. It was not until that cataclysmic event that I realized how much my momentum had slowed. In fact, for a while, I had felt completely immobilized, but I kept ignoring it and postponing the inevitable. Had they not fired me, I can only imagine what other pits I would have fallen into. That was the beginning of my rescue story, but I did not know it because the solution did not seem clear. After all, I was in a foreign land, I had no job, and the one person I thought cared about my well-being had walked away. So, of course, I questioned God. After all, wasn't He the Author and Finisher of everything? So, why did He abandon me? But just in time, God reminded me that He is the Lord, and nothing is too hard for Him. (Jeremiah 32:27).

Little did I know that being sacked was the prelude to a blessing and a rewarding season of my life. God would do what seemed impossible to man and set me on a trajectory of purpose. Out of disappointment often comes opportunity and sometimes even enlightenment. About two months after losing my job, I started attending church regularly. During this season, the theme at church was, "We are more than conquerors." The focus was on Romans chapter 8, and I was particularly taken with verse 28: "And we know that all things work together for good to them that love God, to them who are the called according to His purpose." It was then God gave me the chance of a lifetime, the opportunity to find and live my purpose. God came through for me in a way I had never experienced before. Don't get me wrong, I have always believed in God, but this occurrence renewed my hope and catapulted me into a new understanding of what it means to leave it all up to Him.

As a young girl, growing up in Jamaica, I had always wanted to help people, but I did not have a specific plan for attaining that. This new job set me on a path to work with people experiencing homelessness, and as the cliché says, "I've never looked back." The next seven years would find me serving this population while constantly looking for ways to improve my service. This aligns with Mathew 23:11, reminding us that our servants shall be the greatest among us. Destitution had brought me to life's true meaning—service to humankind rather than self.

As a child, I completely believed in God and did not think anything was impossible. I had many book characters through whom I lived vicariously, and I knew that someday what I imagined would become my reality. Yet, after being knocked down too many times, I found myself believing that's the way life is. This is what happened to me. I did not know the person I had become, but I knew I wanted out. Og Man dino once said, "One of the things is we tend to give up too soon. We get knocked down a couple of times, and we stay down. It's so important to get back up again." I knew that I had to find a way to get up and keep moving because God was not through with me yet.

The experience of being knocked down by life reminded me of my last year in high school. It was filled with so much uncertainty because my mother told me that after high school, she was done with helping me financially. It was not because she was a bad mother. On the contrary, she did what she deemed best for her children, but at that time, I believe she was just tired. She had invested in my three older siblings and felt by then that the return on her investment was not prolific. However, the timing could not have been worse from my vantage point. My hopes were dashed; I had big dreams of continuing my education. I needed to get out of poverty. As far as I knew, this was my only conduit. Hence, my mother's decree complicated things, and I started to experience the onset of hopelessness and helplessness. My mind often wandered to all the prior moments when I was knocked down. Would I get up this time?

Let us take a walk back to the days of my youth. The life I lived growing up and the one I dreamed of was, at best, paradoxical. I was born in a one-bedroom government house in rural Jamaica, where I spent all my childhood. I grew up with six siblings, five of whom lived with my mother and me in that one bedroom. I stayed there until I was sixteen, after which I left home. Life was hard growing up, and I did life hard because I had no choice. In our way, we were happy because we had each other. My father did not live with us, but we visited him often and vice versa. This did not change the fact that we were poor; I was very aware of it. However, from my purview, even as a child, our state of poverty was not permanent. My mother's philosophy on the subject also did much to reassure me. She believed and instilled in us the idea that a solid education alleviates poverty. Therein lived my beacon of hope, and I dwelled there often.

I started reading at two years old, and by the age of ten, I had read all the books my mother stored on her three makeshift bookshelves. Little did I know then that being such an avid reader would open my mind to unknown realities and evoke an undying longing. I knew then that I wanted to be somebody. I wanted to be affluent, and I wanted to live like the ladies in my novels. I admired Maya Angelou and went around reciting "Phenomenal Woman" every chance I got. I believed I was phenomenal! I was diligent and persistent, and education was essential to me. More than anything, I wanted to help people, so I had to become a success.

My reality then was abject poverty, but my dream was affluence and philanthropy. I knew I wanted to help people, especially people like me. My decision was solidified when, at twelve, I was stopped dead in my tracks by someone much stronger than me. I underwent an ordeal that drastically changed who I was, what I thought I could do, and who I could be. Imagine being raped by a pastor who was supposed to protect and reassure. That happened to me, and I blamed myself and my circumstances, even God.

After that traumatic experience, I lost my confidence, hope, trust, and belief in humanity. I became quite reserved and only found solace in the myriad books I read. But one thing that did not die was my zeal to succeed. I became more determined than ever before. My zeal to succeed was a powerful force that drove me to prioritize achieving greatness. It was and still is that burning desire to accomplish my goals and reach my full potential, even in the face of challenges and adversity. This zeal allows me to persevere through setbacks and failures and push toward my dreams. That passion is fueled by the belief that anything is possible with hard work, determination, and a never-give-up attitude. However, it is not just about achieving my personal goals but also about positively impacting the world and leaving a legacy.

Before realizing this, I was stuck in a place of unforgiveness and bitterness for a while. You see, I blamed what happened to me on my circumstances. I thought, *if we weren't poor, this would never have happened.* But, as James Allen says, "Adversity introduces a man to himself." After that, I made a pact to get out of poverty. Education was my outlet. I knew I wanted to help people, and I could not let what happened to me befall anyone else. Not if I could help it.

There is something extremely debilitating about poverty that gets into your head and immobilizes you. If you are not mentally tough, you can sink into its grimy pit at the drop of a hat with no foreseeable escape path. It did not help that I was completely clueless at the time. However, I continued to believe success was possible, no matter what. If others had done it, then maybe, just maybe, I could do it too. My mindset then was if I could think it and I believed it hard enough, I could do it and grow from the experience too.

During my final year of high school, while performing mandatory community service at a law firm, I told the lawyer who ran the firm about my dream to attend the University of the West Indies, the top-ranked University in Jamaica at the time. He quickly told me to be more realistic. It was not likely that I would make it to that institution coming from my high school, he exclaimed. He told me I was aiming too high, and my dreams would be dashed if I did not change that wishful thought. My will to win and my abhorrence for poverty saved me from his myopic mental purview. If only he knew the determination that slept in the deep reservoir of my mind, he would not have uttered such abominable words. It is incredible how enervating even the best intentions can be if one has no inner resolve to resist negativity. My desire to succeed was so strong that my attitude to his words was, "Your opinion is none of my business; that is your business."

He did not know that my determination was greater than my fears; going to university was not a destination for me but a route. I had even bigger dreams, and as my mother had instilled in me from the outset, education was the only way. I believed this completely. I had visions of one day owning a home with detailed stonework and a long driveway, building my mother a home of her own, and leaving a life of poverty. Today, with my help, Mommy has a house of her own. She toiled and sweated for it, and I was able to contribute to that venture, so we know for sure that dreams do come true. I needed to attend university, and no one would tell me differently. The expression, "Stand up for what you believe in," suddenly had meaning to me. There is a marked difference between just saying something and believing what you are saying. A new fire ignited in me then, and I was determined more than ever to keep it alight.

Unfortunately, upon graduation, my parents could not afford to send me to college, so I joined the National Youth Service Corps. I worked for a year and received a stipend which amounted to a paltry sum at best. The following year I went to college despite having no money to pay the tuition. I think this is what the person who created the oxymoron, *blind faith*, was trying to get at. There is no such thing as blind faith however, because the very essence of faith is seeing things as if they are before they happen. What I had was *now faith*, as referenced in Hebrews 11:1. I believed God would make a way, so I enrolled. Many doors were opened and closed before me during this time. But in those lean years, I learned how to survive by working while attending school. I perfected the art of dedication and got accustomed to asking for what I wanted. I asked, believing I would receive it, and in many instances, I did. I understood that hearing "*no*" was not the end of the world but a closer proximity to hearing "*yes*."

So, it should come as no surprise that, after college, I was accepted into the University of the West Indies. I graduated three years later with a Bachelor of Science in Political Science and International Relations, double major. My mother had already planted the seeds of success in my mind. These seeds were watered with determination and persistence. If you defy the laws of nature, your results will be unfavorable. So, while many thought my desires were impossible dreams, I knew they were a natural progression. One of the things I learned during those years is that the mind is more powerful than we can ever imagine. *My dream became a reality through faith, hard work, and an inherent will to win.* This statement is still my mandate, and I am sticking to it!

I have long realized that sometimes even the most chaotic situations can set you on a trajectory to discovering God's will for your life. Purpose seldom ever traverses a straight path. In fact, most people's purpose is only ignited after they have fallen into one form of pit or another. For me, it was the threat of poverty; for some, it is deception, betrayal, abuse, and a litany of other possibilities. But as we often see, pain is a common precursor to purpose. Though I knew then that I wanted to help others, not knowing how I would have been able to do that meant putting this desire off until the opportune time. Meanwhile, life happened.

My mother's cardinal rule to "get an education" was forever etched on my mind and was paramount for me. It meant that I attended school all my life until my late twenties. I acquired multiple degrees, attended law school, became an attorney-at-law, and in 2014, decided that it was time to make a life for myself. I was excited about undertaking the legal practice. By then, I had sent out about fifty job applications and eagerly anticipated the myriad of job offers from which I simply had to choose one. However, I was completely deflated when no one called me back for a job opportunity. I ended up taking on a temporary assignment waiting tables in a restaurant as, somehow, I had to make ends meet.

After all my major accomplishments, I felt unfulfilled and perpetually stuck. Was there a logical explanation for me to feel like a failure? My emotional state successfully defied logic, as I had failed miserably. Worse yet, I felt utterly alone. There was a gnawing lump of anxiety that seemed to persist indefinitely. For years, I felt I was only existing rather than truly living. I was slowly dying, and that was a travesty. So, when my boss called me in and promptly fired me that fateful day in 2016, God had a plan, though I didn't know it then. When I say being fired was a blessing, understand that I needed to be stopped and awakened from my slumber. Like an epiphany, I suddenly understood the longing I had experienced for so many years. It dawned on me that you can accomplish everything others think is amazing, but it means nothing if you are not living *your* purpose. Others constantly told me how accomplished I was, but none of those accolades excited me the way finding my calling did. Having a job that allows me to meaningfully help people is both rewarding and fulfilling.

Today, I am immensely grateful for that frightful day I fell into that pit. I waited nervously there for two months. I thought I was waiting on a job, but God kept me in that pit to give me better than I anticipated. I didn't find a job; I found myself. I still work with the homeless and currently partner with an organization that aims to end poverty and homelessness. I, who was once buried in the pits of poverty, loss, abuse, and hopelessness, have germinated, blossomed, and I am now bearing nutritious fruits. Like the pit of a fruit, God used my dark place to prepare me to grow roots and develop and spread my branches to bless others. I am full of hope, joy, and a resounding belief that all things are possible with God!

Meet Shauna-Kaye Brown

Shauna-kaye Brown is a Christian motivational speaker, transformation coach, attorney-at-law of 9 years, and Vice President of Housing for Community Housing Innovations, a nonprofit organization based in New York, USA. She is also a leadership maven who, through John C. Maxwell and Toastmasters International, has been certified in public speaking, training, and coaching. She leaves an indelible mark in every capacity she works in and has exemplified discipline, tenacity, and commitment in her leadership.

Shauna-kaye is also a #1 Amazon bestselling author specializing in curating personal development books, journals, planners, and notebooks. Her most recent forays into writing resulted in the birth of the Self-Starter Journal series and The Strategic Goalsetting Handbook and Workbook, respectively. These are all sold on Amazon worldwide, along with her other books.

CHAPTER 9

Something Better after Waiting

"Commit your way to the Lord; trust in Him, and He will act." **(Psalm 37:5)**

After completing my degree in social work at San Andres University, I worked in the Truth Neighborhoods and Communities Program in the Autonomous Municipal Government of La Paz in my country, Bolivia, as a social worker. The main objective of this program was to improve the life quality of the population. Even though it was a fulfilling job in terms of the impact, after working for three years, I was not offered a contract renewal, and neither did I request it. I was anticipating other opportunities in another field of interest.

Additionally, I did not find the job gratifying because of the heavy demands. I often had to do overtime in the evenings and work on weekends. I also had to adapt to people's availability, especially in implementing social projects.

Some of my other colleagues did not renew their contracts as well. Most were applying for other jobs, and I thought of doing the same. However, this was not exactly what I desired. I believed it was time to pursue my dream of exploring places I had never seen before in Bolivia with my mother, who had worked long and hard and deserved an adventure.

Before leaving for my travels, I left my resume at a municipal government office. We then traveled for three weeks. When I returned, I realized that my application was denied. What to do next? After much contemplation, I decided this was an opportune time to do something different; but what could it be? Confused about what direction to take and which decision to make, I remembered one of the things my mother practiced since I was a child that I had enjoyed doing with her. I needed to strengthen and align my steps for my next life chapter, so I went to the mountain to fast with a group of brothers and sisters. I embraced this custom and did it on every possible occasion.

The experience of focusing on God, talking to Him, learning more about His Word, and hearing testimonies of how He acts in real life and how the promises in the Bible were being put into practice is indescribable. Whenever I listened to these testimonies, I would say, *If God can do all those things for others, He could and would do it for me.* With each visit, I would be encouraged to get closer to God, so I started going there routinely, and the experience was delightful.

One of the promises I gleaned from these sessions was Jeremiah 33:3: "Call to me and I will answer you and tell you great and unsearchable things you do not know." (NIV) Most of these promises are conditionals, where we need to do something to activate the blessings. In this case, we are invited to call on God. I said, *"Why not practice it?"* I started praying more and made it a habit to fast on Wednesdays.

I had a curiosity to travel overseas on a scholarship. This could be an excellent opportunity to experience two things I like simultaneously: studying and visiting new places. However, I had no idea how to go about it. I started asking around, but no one in my immediate circle had any valuable information to proffer. It seemed like a farfetched goal. Since one of my deep interests was studying, one day, I went to ask for information about a higher education postgrad degree. I had a longstanding interest in working as a professor at a university.

The person giving this information was a philosophical doctor who explained extensively that they had agreements with foreign universities. I asked him if he knew of any scholarships offered to study abroad, and he explained that he was a beneficiary of foreign scholarships and could help me apply for them. In exchange for his expert assistance, I would help with his project of installing a technical educative institution in a town. We met, and he explained and outlined the details to me. After a few days, he told me there was an available secretary position in the doctoral department where he was the coordinator. He said it would be better if I worked there because we could advance his project and search for the scholarship concurrently.

Even though working as a secretary was unrelated to my area of expertise, it was interesting because it was in a well-known and prestigious higher education institution, San Andres University.

The primary purpose was to get help to find a scholarship. I started working as a secretary during the day while helping him with his project, even on Sundays and holidays. I had to travel to a town where his technical educational institution was. It was a sacrifice because I did not have much time, even on the weekends.

When I started working there, I was finishing a postgrad course in public investment projects; then, I started another postgrad in higher education in the evenings. During this time, I could not give adequate attention to searching for a scholarship because I had little time to spare. After finishing this course, I said, *I need to focus on searching for a scholarship because this is the main reason I am there.*

On the one hand, it was interesting to be involved in an academic area with Ph.D. candidates, especially when they defended their thesis with foreign courts. However, I felt dissatisfied and uncomfortable because I thought it was better to work applying the knowledge of what I studied. The work environment could have been better as well.

I refocused and started searching for scholarships during the middays and evenings. I reminded my boss of his commitment to help me apply for a scholarship and our agreement for me to work and help him with his project. He only searched a few times because he was prioritizing his other tasks. So, I needed to make more effort to pursue my dream.

It was a challenging task considering my limited experience. I found few opportunities in the social area. Another difficulty was that, at that time, I only spoke Spanish, the official language of my country. One of the requirements of most of these international

Waiting In the Pit

scholarships was to be an English speaker. I regretted not learning it before.

I could go as far as Europe since most Latin Americans selected Spain because of the language. In addition, it caught my attention when I heard that Europe was a small continent where the countries were close, and once there, you could take advantage of exploring the different countries. I applied online to pursue a course in Spain but was denied. I then applied to universities in Mexico even though I was not overly interested in going there; it did not work out either.

I descended into a pit of discouragement, feeling I would not achieve my dream of acquiring a scholarship. Desperate, I applied to South American countries such as Brazil and Argentina, even though I was not interested in attending any of them. I needed to travel outside of my country, even if it was to a neighboring country. I felt pressed to continue pursuing my dream of traveling and studying overseas, even amid the constant disappointments and denials. I thought these were more accessible opportunities, but the applications were unsuccessful again.

In my despair, I persisted in prayer. I remembered some promises in the Bible, like Joshua 1:9: "Have I not commanded you? Be strong and courageous. Do not be afraid; do not be discouraged, for the Lord your God will be with you wherever you go." (NIV) Life can be full of challenges, regrets, and difficult decisions. But even during difficulties, the Lord advises us to be strong and courageous. Understanding that verse can help us face difficult moments and endure as we wait in our pits of circumstances with faith and trust. Part of striving and being courageous means trusting in the Lord as our trustworthy source of strength.

In Joshua's case, he did not have all the answers to the challenges ahead, but he was counseled to go ahead anyway, acting in faith. Like Joshua, when plunged into our pits of disappointments and delays, we rarely have all the answers, but God promises us that when we turn to Him for guidance, we will succeed. God is omnipotent and omniscient; He has the answers and the strength we need to face any challenge. He was with Joshua when he was in his pit of uncertainty, and we need to believe He is with us when we are in our various pits.

I persevered in the middays and evenings because it was also a way to leave that job. Waiting helped me trust God even when I did not understand what was happening. I deepened my prayer life and developed communion with our Father.

Finally, I found one scholarship for a short training course in Japan organized by Japan International Cooperation Agency (JICA). I could not believe it was to go to Japan because I did not consider Asia a possibility for travel and study, maybe because it was farthest and seemed unattainable. The great news was that the language offered for this course was Spanish. However, the course was not related to my field of study; it was about micro and small businesses.

Nevertheless, I decided to apply because I did not find another scholarship opportunity or offer. The application was through the Bolivian Government. I sought clarification, tried to meet all the requirements, and assembled the folder with all the specifications indicated.

The official told me the next step was waiting for the results. Reviewing the documents would take two stages: first at the national office and then through JICA. After some days, the official called, advising me they needed the signature of someone of maximum authority where I previously worked. Getting that caliber signature from the municipal government meant acquiring it from my city's mayor, which was difficult and impossible in such a short time. Nonetheless, I found a way to get the signature of one of the major authorities, and it was accepted. I nervously yet hopefully waited for the results in the following weeks. Unfortunately, the application was not successful.

It was discouraging because I invested a lot of time and effort and did not get satisfactory results. I sank lower into my pit of despair. In a daze, I watched people having fun after work or during midday, watching movies or going for a walk, eating together, and having a good time. At church, people went to play volleyball, one of my favorite sports, but I was trapped in my pit of despair, unable to see anything but the dark clouds that hovered over my dream. It seems that I was wasting my time on something that was not yielding any positive results.

I said to our Lord, "*Father, it seems I have been praying in vain. Why aren't my applications going through?*" Still, I remembered what I heard in the church about handling disappointments. We should not say, "God, why is this not happening?" Instead, we should ask, "What is the purpose for this situation not working?" or "What better thing do you have that I cannot see or understand now?"

God is sovereign and omniscient. He knows all things from eternity to eternity. Nothing that happens to us surprises Him. We must always trust that if He allows or withholds something in our lives, good or bad, easy or difficult, He will accompany us and help us to overcome the situation or our disappointments. Even when we do not see a clear solution, our faith must be placed only in God and His goodness during those circumstances.

Waiting, though painful, positioned me to reflect on how God worked in the past. I remembered some experiences when I wanted something, and it seemed as if I did my best and persevered in prayer, but it did not work out. However, after a short period, I got something better, and I understood that I needed only to trust God because He had His purpose on it. Those experiences assured me that He is always working in my favor. This confirms one of Ellen White's quotes, "I have nothing to fear for the future unless I forget how God has led me in the past." Also, while I waited in my pit of anxiety and despair, I remembered that God acts in His time. He has perfect timing; it is never early, and it is never late. God is never in a hurry because He is always on time.

I determined to trust in God that He is in control because He knows what is happening and knows the best option. I was thinking and praying that I should change my plan and apply for a course here in Bolivia instead of searching the internet for scholarships. However, I decided to try one more time. I would change the plan or direction if it did not work again. After a few days, I found another scholarship for a short training course in Japan, "Rural Development through Life Improvement Approach for Latin America," organized by JICA, and the language was Spanish. This time, the course was related to my field of study.

I was enthusiastic about applying there because it was the same institution I had applied to prior, so the format to present the folder was the same, just a different emphasis. It was easier to meet the requirements because the job experience and some postgrad courses I took were related to that. Everything was going well. As with the previous experience, I had to wait for the results after I presented the folder to the government office. After approximately one month, one of the JICA officials called me, asking for some details. A few days later, they called me again to say, "Congratulations! You won the fully funded scholarship for the training course." I was glad to hear that, even though it was for a short training course.

I thanked God wholeheartedly. I now saw why the previous institutions did not accept me because this last opportunity was the best. The wait now made sense. The application to Japan was not related to my field of study. If they had accepted me, I would have had to make a lot of effort studying and trying to understand that field. I would be required to propose a project, and when I returned to Bolivia, I would have to apply it.

However, this course made it easy to understand, and I could propose, explain, and apply the project seamlessly. Moreso, the experience was interesting. Additionally, with the first application, I would only have gone to Japan. But with this one, I had the opportunity to visit Japan, Mexico, and the Dominican Republic for at least one week to learn how people who took the same course previously were applying the knowledge acquired. My blessing tripled.

I said, *"Thank you, Father! Thank you for saying no prior."* I was reminded again very practically that His plans are better than mine and His ways are higher. As Isaiah 55:8-9 says, "For as the heavens are higher than the earth, so are my ways higher than your ways, and my thoughts than your thoughts." Think about how difficult it is to understand the reasoning of others who think differently from you. If people's minds differ, imagine how different the human mind is compared to a complex, all-knowing, and sovereign God.

Our thoughts are controlled by emotions and circumstances that we often cannot regulate or control. That is why we must trust in God, who knows everything. He sees the whole story and guides us accordingly. Sometimes our emotions lower us into pits of anxiety and despair. Other times, our circumstances thrust us into a pit of sorrow and disappointments, but in these moments, we are really in the pit of God's hand, being prepared for greater!

Let's trust that God knows the reasons behind our delays and disappointments. I am still learning to wait on the Lord, to trust Him under challenging circumstances, and use these opportunities to develop a closer walk with Him. I now see my pits as a waiting room where I get to spend valued time with Him, assess and do self-work, and find peace in praise. Even when sometimes it seems that He is taking too long, I trust there is a purpose in the wait, and He is preparing me for better.

In Psalm 131, David advises God's children to wait. "Wait, O Israel, on Jehovah." One of the secrets of the great victories the Lord had granted him was to master the "wait."

While waiting in your pit, look up and know that the God of David and Israel is yours. God fulfilled the promise He made to them. In my situation, He gave me better than I anticipated. With you, it will not be less. Therefore, do not be discouraged. Trust God with all your heart, knowing He sees our tears, feels our pain, and hears our every cry. God can and will turn your test into a testimony and your trials into triumph. Let us allow Him to lead us. Submit to God's plan and let His will be done.

Meet Yanet Ruth Guarachi

Yanet Ruth Guarachi is a Christian from Bolivia. God is her Father and her best friend. She is a social worker with a Master's in Scientific Research. She enjoys traveling, reading, writing, singing, learning, teaching, sharing God's Word, and developing friendships.

She served in the church as children's teacher, church secretary, treasurer, guide in Pathfinders Club, and women's ministry secretary. She currently is the children's ministry director. She would like to continue serving God as a missionary in different countries wherever the Lord leads, desiring God's will to be done in her life.

As a social worker, she worked in family, groups, and community, developing the functions of social assistance, education, management, research, organization, and promotion. In the formal education area. She has taught at the university, institutes, and high schools.

She can be contacted at **ruth.guarachi1@gmail.com**

CHAPTER 10

Pit of Shame and Unforgiveness

*"Humble yourself in the sight of the Lord and he shall lift you up." **(James 4:10)***

I don't remember all the events of my childhood, but specific details are etched in my memory. My fondest recollection was being around my auntie, my uncle's wife, on my father's side. She was a teacher of manners who always corrected my grammar and wanted me to have her grand piano. Things didn't work in my favour, and I never got it. This marked one of my first life disappointments, but it paled compared to the challenges I would face throughout my life.

My early childhood years were spent living with my extended family of aunties, uncles, cousins, grandma, and grandpa. This house was always brimming, and a fragrance of excitement permeated the atmosphere. My cousins and I slept on the living room floor on used clothes called 'bedding.' We kept worship in the house on Friday evenings at sunset, and Sabbath lunch was a special feature prepared on Fridays because we were Seventh Day Adventists. I had great moments living with my relatives, but it wasn't the haven it appeared to be.

I became very domesticated, and many of the tasks in the household were assigned to me, and sometimes I was overworked. Additionally, I was exploited by someone who should have been my protector. At a tender age, I was touched inappropriately by my grandfather. It cast a gloom over my childhood, and I never told another soul about it. I wished with all pure desire from a child's heart that he would disappear. During that tender age, my mum was not living with us but came to visit with some white people she worked for. I remember her always looking well-dressed whenever she visited.

At age eight, my mother gave birth to a little boy and brought him to my grandparents' place for my aunt to care for. My aunt wasn't excited about this assignment. When she saw my baby brother, she scorned him. "Too white and small," she scoffed. From that point on, I cared for him in every way possible. I even did his chores when he was old enough to be assigned tasks. I sometimes thought my brother was sometimes illtreated, and I did everything to shield him. I was my brothers' keeper and protector.

Living at my grandparent's home had many challenges, and the food was never enough. I remembered searching through the garbage for food many times at school. One day during my search, I found a cockroach. Unfortunately for me, other children witnessed this discovery, and from there on, I was labelled the 'cockroach girl.' The cook may have heard them teasing, took pity, and started feeding me. God sent an angel to rescue me. I could also feel the love from my teachers and the cooking staff. They even gave me seconds if I wanted more. This was a true blessing.

Sometimes my mother came and took me to her job. She was a domestic worker who did babysitting and cleaning for a white family. I benefited from being around this family as they gave me their hand-me-downs. These second-hand clothing appeared very new to me and smelled good.

Finally, my mum came to live with us in a downstairs apartment at my grandparents' house, which my uncle owned. As far as I can remember, we stayed there briefly. We were evicted because the family felt my mum was bringing a man into the house. This was not true because I can never recall my mum bringing a guy there.

We had nowhere to go until my cousin, who lived not too far off on squatting or government land, got us a piece of the property, and we built a one-room galvanized house. It was home because I was happy and peaceful, living with my mum and brother. Despite our lack, it was a small window in my childhood where I can say I was truly happy.

At around age ten, my mum met a gentleman, and that connection changed my entire life. He was a builder and rebuilt the galvanized house into a wooden structure. The house was bigger, with a living room, bedrooms, kitchen, and even an outhouse. This should have made my life more comfortable, but the discomfort he brought was unbearable for a little girl.

Although he elevated us physically and financially, this man became the bane of my childhood. His feet created a forbidden

Pit of Shame and Unforgiveness

path to my bedroom, where he visited at night and even in the daytime to sexually abuse me. I hadn't a clue what molestation or sexual abuse was then, but I wasn't happy about what was happening to me. In the same manner that I knew what my grandfather was doing was wrong, I knew this man had no right sneaking into my room and touching me. I often dropped hints to my mum to tell her what he was doing to me, but she didn't pay attention. It became unbearable that I didn't want to be home when he was there. I felt utterly trapped in a pit of shame for many years.

Around age 15, I requested an audience with Mum and revealed everything. Her disappointing response was, "He is the breadwinner of the family." She eventually approached him about it, and he denied it, saying he came into the room to spray mosquitoes. My mother bought that excuse lock, stock, and barrel.

She didn't want to accept that she was with a molester or criminal and be without a man's comfort and help. I had no reason to tell lies about this man. I recall feeling his hand touching me when he entered my room; I would jump up, then he would crawl back out. This went on for years, from a man my mother loved, trusted, and welcomed into her family. Only God knows how much I hated him and the disgust I felt, but I kept silent. My mum never understood my course attitude and why I never wanted to be home.

Church activities kept me occupied, but the enemy would also interrupt my peace at church. After a while, my mother gave birth to a little girl, and church people thought she was mine. Where

Waiting In the Pit

was the big belly to prove pregnancy? I don't know! A seed of lie was planted, and church people started gossiping about me. They said all manner of things because I came from the ghetto. I didn't know or understand the word promiscuity, but that label was attached to my reputation because I was a jovial and friendly person. These church people knew nothing about me and what I was facing at home. There were times I constantly told my mum that she didn't like me (I would never use the word love because I didn't feel it at all). My mother chose a man over her child. To this day, he is my mother's husband. This reality sank me into a pit of disappointment and pain for years.

I also lived in a pit of fear and torment, and no one offered to cast a rope to pull me out. On the contrary, they kicked dirt and stones at me in my pit. In addition to the molestation, I suffered much ridicule at home and was referred to as "Susie, the maid." I only wanted to find a place to be loved and accepted. Unfortunately, the church did not supply the love I needed.

Despite the darkness surrounding my life at home and the shame I was carrying, I maintained a cheerful and light spirit, believing God would rescue me. I prayed for His love one day, and graciously, He sent it to me. He heard my cry and saved me from that man who became my mother's husband. I prayed and told Him I was ready for happiness and got it!

Meeting my husband was the best thing to have ever happened to me. He brought the happiness, security, and love I had desired for years. God granted me my longing and gave me a unique family, my very own family. Our union bore two sons. People looked at our family and often commented that it was ideal. But jealousy

Pit of Shame and Unforgiveness

and envy penetrated our unity. Folks felt jealous of our relationship and his genuine love for me.

My husband valued my submissive way as I never did anything without letting him know or went anywhere without informing him. I was very transparent and crowned him with respect. We lived to please God and each other. I thought I was not good enough for him because of how his family operated. They didn't like me because I lacked education, and they resented my origin, better known as the ghetto/bad area. Nevertheless, my dear husband stuck by my side; he helped to educate, support, and comfort me. I was always his "babe," his number one after God, but the Devil laid snares and formed weapons against us.

My family life was well respected; everyone looked up to us. You would ask, what went wrong? When you are working and love the Lord, it upsets the Devil. Demonic forces entered our home through different entities. (Be careful who and what you allow into your home.) I was lied to and always had to defend myself. I always felt I was in trouble. Life was sometimes so burdensome, and the thing is, it wasn't my family that burdened me, but outside forces. Church members were the coldest and meanest to me. Many who claimed to be spiritual were carnally minded and inflicted the most hurt. Tons of stone, debris, and dirt were shovelled at me in my pit.

Singing was my passion, and I found comfort in singing and learning songs. Personal ministry was our family's top priority, so we went from place to place, ministering to different people. Unfortunately, my marriage did not survive the many attacks. I was divorced at age 45 by a force I couldn't explain and wasn't able to control.

Before our separation, I was told by my son that he had an encounter with demons talking to him, telling him that our family was shattered and that they got his father wrapped. I told my husband what my son said and pleaded with him for us to unite in prayer because demons had infiltrated the home. He responded, "What is our son doing talking to demons?" He didn't heed the warning, and the attacks were too much for me to fight alone.

Due to the length constraints for this chapter, I can't share all the details of what took place in my pits of marital and familial disintegration; I may have to capture it in an entire book. However, I survived the bitter battles, and I'm grateful God has given me another chance and the opportunity to tell my story. He delivered me from a lifelong series of pits, hurt, shame, and disappointments. Going through molestation, neglect by the one who was supposed to protect me, enduring sexual harassment from family members, being ridiculed by church members, and suffering troubles of every dimension propelled me into a person who was very defensive, fearful, and unable to trust anyone. All these led to suicidal thoughts. I felt hopeless, but God became my escape. He alone understood and saw the various pits I had fallen in all my life, comforting me while I languished in them.

God always wanted me. Through His strength, I could ignore and operate as if I didn't hear what others said about me. I always believed that there was a God in my deepest pits because I constantly cried out to Him. God revealed Himself multiple times.

Pit of Shame and Unforgiveness

In dreams, he showed me the state of my life and assured me He would not forsake me. I thank God for not abandoning me.

I suffered a lot in my early years because there wasn't anyone to reach out to for genuine support. I thought I could find support among church people. However, I didn't. When church folk hurt you, it's a deep, deep hurt because of the expectation that they should be God's representative on earth. I learned the hard way that God is the only One who we can truly depend on, and I resolved to be the person who would be there for others. I was always a person who genuinely looked out for the well-being of others, but for me, there was a lack. Alone in my pit, I often hummed:

"Pass me not, oh gentle Saviour!

Hear my humble cry,

While on others, Thou art calling

Do not pass me by...."

These words would saturate my mind and give me comfort. Also:

"When peace like a river attendeth my way

When sorrows like seas billows roll

Whatever my lot, thou hast thought me to say,

'IT IS WELL, IT IS WELL, WITH MY SOUL.'"

Like Joseph, who was tossed in a pit, God became my solace and sent deliverance.

I signed up for a program called "Celebrating Life in Recovery," spearheaded by Sherry Peters. Through this program, I had the privilege to meet and talk with her on Zoom. She used the book *Steps to Christ* in a recovery form. This program was introduced to me by a dear cousin. The program changed my life and came right on time.

God placed my cousin in my life when I needed someone to talk with and go through this journey. This is a cousin who lived in Florida, whom I didn't know very well. I saw her only twice in my life, and I often wished that she would appear again. She did! God did that just for me. She has since moved back home to Trinidad. Praise God! He did it for me; He is crazy about me. He didn't leave me alone in my pit to languish but sent support and comfort when I needed it most.

In this program, I learned the following:

1. Nothing is too difficult for God to do for me. God never leaves; we leave Him. God will do anything to help us once we want it, but first, we must forgive ourselves and others.

2. Character transformation is based on a relationship with God through which He transforms us. So, when we go to God, our Source, He will furnish our souls.

3. We need to guard what we watch. "Guard the avenues of our souls" and who we entertain.

4. Set a time for bed and get ample rest. Let God be the last voice we hear at night.

5. We need to be spiritually minded. Focus on God and feed upon spiritual things. Memorizing the Scriptures helps.

6. Vigilantly socialize and be the friend you desire in others.

7. Turn away from addictions (SINS). "If we confess our sins, he is faithful and just to forgive us our sins, and to cleanse us from all unrighteousness." (1 John 1:9)

My prayer life transformed and became more meaningful. It was now based on my needing Jesus and acknowledging what He has done for me. Additionally, God showed me where I needed to pray for myself and others more. Through a friend's devotion, it was shown to me that God is with me and wants to reveal Himself to me. I stuck close to God as He removed the defects in my character. I was out of control at times, not restraining my temper. But I asked God to help me to communicate love. God's power, Holy Spirit, and being born again strengthened me. From this seed planted in my pit moment, I grew like a beanstalk out of my pit.

By surrendering my life day by day, things have gotten better. Satan was distracting me by using sadness and sorrow to consume me, but I learned to crucify myself and focus on Christ. I was always considered to be a strong, vibrant, full of laughter-person, and I reclaimed my joy because the Word said:

"To appoint unto them that mourn in Zion, to give unto them beauty for ashes, the oil of joy for mourning, the garment of praise for the spirit of heaviness; that they might be called trees of righteousness, the planting of the Lord, that He might be glorified." (Isaiah 61:3)

Jesus is my rescuer! He has redeemed and delivered me from my pits of hurt, unforgiveness, disappointment, and pain, and given me a new start. I have forgiven those who have offended me, and I am looking forward to better days. I am still a work in progress, growing, thriving, and bearing fruit for His kingdom. If I could grow out of my pit of shame and disappointment, so can you. Feed on the Word of God, and allow Him to water and nurture your soul, and you will overcome your life's pits.

He did it for me; He can do it for you too!

Meet Carlene Peters

Carlene Peters is a beautiful soul from the twin island of Trinidad and Tobago. She is the mother of two god-fearing boys who are talented singers. She is a very committed mom who tries to live a balanced life with God as her guide.

She is very passionate and jovial about everything and anything life gives. She has the gift of planning events, networking, and interacting with others. She loves singing and tries to make a conscious effort to put others first. She has a passion for ministry and loves serving others.

Carlene is the proud owner of a janitorial company. She possesses certificates in childcare and gerontology. She holds a BSc in Behavioral Science.

Her greatest desire is to see men and women come to Christ and be saved in God's kingdom.

CHAPTER 11

Pit of Alienation

"I love the LORD, because he hath heard my voice and my supplications." **(Psalms 116:1)**

After I had been writhing and squirming for two years in the great depression of a very disorienting and distracting marital separation, my wife died suddenly, leaving me behind alone to contend with the unforeseen miry and mirky depths of the pit of blame, suspicion, and alienation. She had not been ill. She had not overdosed on pills or died in a vehicular accident, but she had been strangely murdered—viciously and brutally stabbed to death at the hand of a ruthless, mysterious assailant, just minutes after arriving home from church.

In the aftermath, many people invariably calculated that I might have had something to do with her death. Perhaps I had acted out of desperate and jealous rage and had taken her life. For some, the fact that a specific killer had not been apprehended simply lent more force to this assumption.

"So, where were you?" queried one total stranger the morning following the incident. She had just obtained my number and sought to get to the bottom of the case before anyone else. It would go to her distinguished credit for hearing from the horse's mouth. After politely accommodating her query, sharing my whereabouts with her, and receiving an ambiguous pronouncement of sympathy, I was depressed and in no mood to talk with anyone else.

For a while, my cell phone rang unanswered. My thoughts were too many to process in a hyperactive space, so I retired to my regular prayer spot, leaving the callers and worriers grappling with the past night's events. My brother, who had a clearer head at the moment said, "Bro... your wife was murdered, you know; she didn't just die a normal death. You cannot afford not to answer your phone. That will only raise questions."

Another onslaught of messages and calls awaited, but I at least had the fortitude of the Spirit of God to help me face them. One family member telephoned from abroad: "Be careful about what you say to the police," he said. "They have a way of twisting what you say to use against you, and they can lock you up and throw away the keys to make you lost in the system." Other people echoed similar concerns. *Why*, I asked myself, *would I ever need to be cautious about what I said to the police? Innocence needs no defense!* What did I have to hide? In my mind, the only cause I would have had for hiding and exercising caution would have been if I had been involved.

Then my mind concluded its relatively slow mathematical processes. Could it be that these people, however well-intentioned, were insinuating my probable guilt and trying to shield me from possible incarceration? The local news was always saturated with stories of domestic crime. The notion was not entirely far-fetched.

The surge of subtle accusations kept mounting. However, one of my wife's coworkers was blatant, "Mr. Lowe, if I ever discover that it was you...!" She left the latter outcome unspoken, perhaps hoping I would live in dread of its suspenseful import. Others took to social media. My Facebook messages spiked as people took pokes while assuming shadow identities, sending messages of accusation, and then withdrawing from view. In the aftermath of my wife's death, the traffic of incoming friend requests went through the roof, and I accepted all of them. People naturally wanted to view images of the candidates in their discussions, and I obliged.

After issuing a personal statement of mourning on my profile, an acquaintance messaged, "Be careful about what you post..." Unwittingly, the seeds of suspicion had planted themselves. It was at first rumored that I had been on the run, but this was probably because I had accidentally left my phone behind on the morning of that fateful day as I hurried off to meet an appointment with my music ministry. To reach me, some folks began speculating whether I had taken flight. But, as it turned out, with the absence of my phone, I had been the last person within my group to have heard about the murder. Not knowing whether I had foreknowledge, they had a real challenge in deciding how best to break the news to me. Imaginations were rampant, and theories abounded in the absence of defined facts and revelations of truth.

Pit of Alienation

At the crime scene, a pivotal side story had unfolded. An officer of the law with whom my wife had been presently involved had shown up and ventured to enter her car. I had called out to him openly and thus prevented him from carrying out what I imagined as possible tampering with damning evidence inside the vehicle. Fears had subsequently arisen that this officer and his affiliates might be interested in harming me for having thus exposed him.

There was uneasy tension on the sides of both families as the funeral service drew near. Being sympathetic to the loss felt by the in-laws, I willingly waived my legal right to the bulk of my wife's possessions. However, I was compelled to judiciously withhold further generosity after learning that they had been actively circulating that I had been the culprit. Any additional disbursement or allowance from me was not to be misconstrued as an act of consolation done out of guilt. They had lost a blood relative. I had lost a rib. She was my flesh. The magnitude of her loss was mutually felt.

To maintain sanity, for the next five weeks, I threw myself at planning the funeral arrangements. I placed myself where I could obtain the most comfort and consolation—right in front of my piano. Yes, I played at my wife's funeral. If I didn't do it, I would have been destroyed inside. This arrangement disconcerted many family members. "Why don't you allow someone else to play?" they urged. They would have preferred that I take a more cautious approach to the event, but I had not done anything, and I had no intention of defending myself from any potential incoming attacks. There was to be no hired security detail. My protection was entirely in the hands of the Almighty. Failing to prevail, many chose to maintain a healthy radius away from me for the duration of the event. Rumors of pending violent eruptions were prevalent, and they were taking no chances, and I was being cautioned to watch my back.

With an air of conscious innocence and the utmost confidence in the power of God, I carried through with my honorable duty without flinching. I was advised that some of the in-laws had been adamant that there would be repercussions if I showed up at the burial site. But even there, God used special circumstances to deflect and mitigate such occurrences. As the final burial rites were being carried out, I was momentarily distracted by a commotion. A young lady had fainted, and an attending colleague came to get me to help in offering her first aid assistance. Together we employed a special hand lift and safely conveyed her to the back of a motor car. Two young men who had been previously trying to assist were thereafter curious to learn the technique we employed to carry the patient. After briefly demonstrating and teaching the method to them, we conversed about the tragic circumstance that had brought about the solemn occasion. It turned out they were both my wife's cousins.

I identified myself as "the husband," sharing with them my dealings with her and how I had lovingly sought after her. Still, she had always adamantly insisted on remaining separated and pursuing alternatives. One commented, "Hmmm. That is why it is always good to hear two sides of a story."

Notwithstanding that the funeral ceremonies had been conducted without incident; I was somewhat mindful of flair-ups. If, in people's minds, I was the guilty culprit, I needed to be wary. Left alone and under very different circumstances, I would have opted to migrate then. I really felt the need to be away from my hometown. I needed fresh air. But I also could not be comfortable with the idea that my family might become targeted in my absence. I, therefore, determined that if there were to be any incoming fire, I would stick around to face it personally. So rather than migrate to click a refresh button on my life, I remained on the home soil. I enrolled in a local university to pursue further studies and regularly visited my parents' home.

I sometimes wonder whether I had made the right choice. I had voluntarily chosen a pit of self-sacrifice and self-denial, considerably narrowing the circle of possibilities. My life might have been better if I had gone away, but I avoided this move because of concern for my family's safety. I could not bear being away only to receive news of mishaps. But I praise God for His beneficent love, grace, mercy, and power to have preserved us safe over the last ten years since my wife's passing. No violence has been directed at me or my family, even though the murderous culprit has not been identified or apprehended.

Still intent on maintaining a helpful presence with my family, I eventually moved back into the hometown sphere in 2018 to live with them. On a busy Sunday morning in 2023, when a high-profile wedding was scheduled, as I agitated with due diligence trying to exit the house to attend a musical event in the capital city, my parents were inside the kitchen. As I hurriedly removed my car keys from the rack, Mom asked, "Are you off to attend the wedding?"

"Oh no," I replied. "I haven't been contracted to play at a wedding in this town for the last ten years."

Dad contributed, "Oh, they (probably) have enough musicians to go around."

"No, Dad," I said. "People haven't invited me to play because they think I killed Tee." Before her passing, I played actively at weddings and other events.

There was mutual silence between them. I knew it to be true because I had experienced a bit of hostility, having been excluded or removed from a few guest lists and, even in the immediate aftermath of my wife's death, been personally ejected from a reception venue. Even efforts at courtship were, for a time, met with censorship and heavy filtering. A big caution sign seemed to hover about my head. I walked freely on the streets, but I existed in a pit of loneliness where only friends and family visited.

I continued, "You'd have to live in my shoes and look through my eyes to see it." My response came as a 'drops mic' moment because, with that, I was out the door. The next day, Mom shared that after I had left, she and Dad had discussed what I had said. They had not been aware that I had been so burdened by the accusations over the years.

"Son," she said, "your father and I long discussed what you said. We believe you need to go away. Get yourself a new start. This place isn't good for you."

At that moment of pronouncement, I suddenly got an epiphany. I was finally free. The word of release had come. God had spoken through my parents, assuring me that it was safe for me to leave them alone. They would be alright. Just like an angel had appeared to the parents of Jesus in Egypt to inform them that those who had sought the Child's life had died, the Lord had caused my parents to pronounce unambiguously that I was finally free to pursue life and live for myself.

I have sat in this pit of alienation privately and patiently. No one before reading this article has ever known why I have remained in my hometown, appearing to have no interest in being anywhere else. Even though I had been abroad on several occasions, these trips were never announced because I always tried to remain unpredictable and anonymous with my whereabouts. But God knew. He understood, and He has shown that He has more in store for me, and by His divine schedule, He has granted permission for my free roaming.

Without bitterness and resentment toward anyone, I have chronicled the events of my life in a book titled *Truth Be Told*. Still, this little bit I have shared of my social incarceration remains exclusive to this publication. As Joseph had in Egypt waited faithfully upon the Lord for his deliverance from the prisoner's pit, I will continue to trust God to bring me to that happy ending He has in store for me. I pray that my related experiences will inspire others to wait patiently upon the Lord; He delivers.

Meet Miguel Lowe

Miguel Lowe is a Jamaican musician, composer, and author. He is a former educator, having taught Music and Geography at primary and high school levels, and is presently involved with emergency and disaster relief services. He is also the Director of Music for Chrysolites Ministries (Jamaica). He has published two books on Amazon.com: **Teach Yourself Piano** and **Flat Earth Fallacy**. His autobiography, **Truth Be Told**, will be released mid to late 2023.

CHAPTER 12

My Pit Stop

"But we have not a high priest which cannot be touched with the feeling of our infirmities; but was in all points tempted like as we are yet without sin." **(Hebrews 4:15)**

We are delighted when life is at its best, but when challenges come, we give in to complaints, doubts, and fear. Sickness is a challenge that deteriorates the physical body and impacts our minds and spiritual growth. It saps us of our energy, drains us emotionally, and plunges us into pits of despair, sorrow, and grief.

We cannot possibly gain spiritual strength without God's transforming power. Often, God uses challenges and circumstances to pave the way to transform and mold our character. Sickness is one of the channels He uses to capture our attention. The beauty of the love of God, however, is that His mercies are beyond limits. Therefore, no matter how many beatings, battering, or bruising life inflicts or how many times illness crashes into us, His grace is sufficient to heal and deliver.

Waiting In the Pit

Like Joseph, our pits and prisons are prerequisites for our promotion to the palace. This is where we are molded and fashioned, learning to depend entirely on God. God never let us go through our dark, unpleasant, and prolonged experiences without learning something to improve our lives.

I can relate to the character of Joseph in many ways. Joseph was known to be a dreamer, and so was I. I have always had dreams since I was a child. Some were scary, and I thought they were evoked by the creepy movies I watched immediately before bedtime. However, there were dreams I had which played out significantly in my life, and I had to just thank God. I am convinced that God gifted me with discernment through my dreams, and I have experienced His guiding protection through revelations over me and my daughter. Some of my dreams are repetitive, and the Lord has revealed the significance of such dreams.

I have learned to value my dreams and depend on God's direction and revelation for the ones I don't understand. In 2020, I dreamt my daughter, Deneve, and I were standing at a bus stop. It appeared to be in the countryside with many rocks, bushes, and stony roads. We waited a while for a bus to arrive.

A bus finally came and stopped at our feet. Many other people were also waiting to board the bus, and within minutes, it was packed to capacity. There were no more seats left for us, so we had to go to the back of the bus, where two coaches were attached. We climbed in and tried to find comfortable seats, but there were none. We were alone on that coach. The ride was very rough, and the coach felt like it would detach from the bus. It swung from side to side as we traversed rough roads and rocky terrain and went up a treacherous hill. Petrified, I turned to Deneve and said, "Learn to drive because of the rocks." I did not know what the Lord wanted to show me at the time, but not long after, in 2021, the message was revealed.

The dream was a premonition for the rough times we were to face. In 2021, I sustained a spinal cord injury. I fell on a stationary exercise bicycle which twisted my body, causing damage to the lumbar region of the spine and the neck. There was a significant shift in my spinal cord. This was an extremely traumatic experience where I endured excruciating physical pain, sorrow, and emotional stress for months before medical treatment. I always feared being sick to the point where I could do nothing for myself unless aided. I was face to face with the very thing I always dreaded. Sometimes our greatest fears manifest themselves to test our faith in trusting God's hands of mercy.

There was severe pain in my neck, back, knees, and entire spine. Painkiller tablets seemed useless and insignificant to the measure of pain I was experiencing. The pain penetrated my bones every two hours, and my body weakened. It would burn as if red pepper was placed in my bone cavities. I started wondering if God had forgotten me. I had to learn new ways of getting on and off the bed, and I had challenges walking and sitting. There was never a comfortable spot to sleep in my bed, so the wheelchair became my solace. My nights were fraught with sleepless and miserable moments. Hot and cold water became my only reprieve, and as my body got used to them, they were no longer satisfying.

In all my suffering, I remembered the benefits of peace from worshipping God. Worship was my balm because I knew wondrous and miraculous things could happen. My greatest life goal is to ensure that my house is always a house of worship. Exodus 23:25 states, "Worship the Lord your God, and his blessing will be on your food and water. I will take away sickness from among you." (NIV) My mother (deceased) maintained that there should always be morning and evening worship to keep the presence of the Holy Spirit in the house, and I have enjoyed its benefits. My mother would be up at 4:00 a.m. having her worship before she called family worship, then we went to separate businesses, whether school or work.

I saw the benefits of having a worship experience with Jesus as I followed her example. I saw the importance of connecting to God in the morning's wee hours as there are fewer distractions and more concentration on God. I have gained and am still gaining from a wonderful worship experience as I consult God at 2 a.m. daily.

When God is about to bless or has blessed us, the old Devil always rears his ugly head, trying to thwart God's plan for our lives. I had just published my first book, *Encouragement: A Source of Strength for Life's Journey*, and was ready to ease into the field of social work, which was always my desire. My life was going on a satisfying and fulfilling path, and I was already considering writing another book in a few months. This book was inspirational, encouraging people to keep positive in life's way, but here I was, very ill and distressed and needed all the encouragement possible. Little did I know that God's plan was manifesting in my life, and I was at a pit stop where He was molding my character and increasing my faith in Him.

Sickness is not a product of God. Job was afflicted with illness and painful sores by the enemy. The Devil uses this type of calamity to discourage individuals and incite doubt. After he waited and passed the test, God blessed Job with more than he had before: possessions and spiritual growth. In my pain, I remember asking God if He had forgotten me. It seemed as if the more I prayed, the more the pain intensified. New treatments were tried, and old remedies explored, but the pain worsened, and inflammation was now setting in. Each night seemed like trepidation. I got no sleep, and each hour was spent languishing for a miracle.

As if that pain was not enough, a new injury was inflicted on my body. I had tied a belt to the grill of my bedroom window to ease myself from the bed, which caused a new injury to my clavicle. Added injury increased the suffering, which worsened as the days progressed, but I maintained my worship sessions with God.

I had an appointment to see an orthopedic specialist within three months. The waiting list was long, and I was nowhere close to the top. I knew I could not possibly wait for three months to get help because my body was deteriorating rapidly. My emotional strength diminished, and I felt I was wasting away. I felt like God was preparing me for the close of my time. I was not even near retirement age, and here I was, crippled—emotionally and physically. I cried out to God for healing. I sought strength in 2 Kings 20:5 "…I have heard your prayer and seen your tears; I will heal you." I needed healing and strength from God desperately.

Isaiah 40:29, "He gives strength to the weary and increases the power of the weak." (NIV) I cried out to God, *"God!!!! I need healing; please hear my cry."*

My God did not forsake me, but it felt like it. Crying became a ritual, and my mind on a marathon, trying to determine what wrong I had committed to cause this trial in my life. I then began to justify that I deserved what I was experiencing. As I lamented, something deep within told me that God was not yet done with me. He would extend complete physical, emotional, and spiritual healing in His perfect time.

I was in the racing car pit for him to repair damages I had incurred over the years. I needed proper servicing, and he needed to retrofit me with parts to take me on the next leg of my journey. I had to learn patience, endurance, forgiveness, gentleness, and other fruits of the Spirit.

God allowed me to stay in this pit of pain and suffering for six months to mold my character. He was trying to get my attention on one particular part, which was critical to the engine of my spiritual vehicle. Two of my spiritual cables were damaged: forgiveness of others and forgiveness from God. Matthew 6:15 admonishes, "But if you do not forgive others… then your Heavenly Father will not forgive your trespasses." (NIV)

Forgiveness is vital in life. We must forgive our fellow men to gain forgiveness from God. Yes, I was going through a period of my life where I had experienced several family collisions. There were several layers of tension between my family members, and forgiveness had to take place for spiritual growth. God did not just want to fix my bones through a surgical procedure; He wanted to help me understand two-fold forgiveness. He wanted me to endure a process so He could repair and service my character to excel on my spiritual journey.

In life's journey, there will be trouble and distress, especially in the ending era. We will experience situations where close friends, family members, co-workers, and the church family will say and do things to hurt us. The hurt can be so extreme that we may feel like avoiding the people who hurt us and moving on, forgetting them altogether. But is it that easy? I always wondered why people hurt others even when they have no reason.

Hurt, especially when being accused wrongfully, impacts heavily on the heart of the accused. My hurt was deep and debilitating. I was falsely accused by people who were close to me, and as a result, I was enveloped with an unforgiving spirit. I felt I could not forgive them for all they had done and were still doing to me. I cried intensely because I had no control over what was happening to me. I remember I cried to God, asking Him why He allowed others to accuse me wrongfully and not allow people looking on to observe the truth. I felt I needed to retaliate seriously, and many times, I sinned even in my very thoughts because of the sly and sarcastic remarks passed about me. I was mistreated and became bitter. This bitterness eroded my core; it was like I had poured oil or some other useless substance into my gas tank, and it damaged my auto-system.

Each time I thought I forgave, I found myself wanting justice. I was walking around with an acidic and poisonous unforgiving spirit. I asked the Lord to forgive me of my sins, but how could

God possibly forgive me in my state of unforgiveness? I could not strive spiritually or otherwise. The two–fold repair work of forgiveness is intense. It is a process of healing that comes with a daily death to the unforgiving spirit. God gives us guidelines and principles in His Holy Scriptures as we journey. He establishes the typical lifestyle to guide our way into the path where He can repair our broken parts. He wants to purify us, create a clean heart, and renew a right spirit within us, and sometimes He must stop us in our tracks, even if it means immobilizing us. My spinal injury was a bitter blessing. Excruciating but restorative.

As I languished physically, my daughter could not bear the sight of my agony and tears. She started researching to find a doctor who could see me in a shorter time than three months. She finally identified a chiropractor whom we got an earlier date for assessment. In less than two weeks, I sat in the chiropractor's office. I was sent to do an MRI, and treatment began thereafter. The chiropractor's intervention was gradual. It was uncomfortable at times but relieving. I listened to my bones crack back into place as the bone mechanic expertly pulled and popped my bones. I was also being cracked and popped spiritually. God impressed upon my heart during my moments of immobility that I needed to release the poisonous substances that were eating at my soul's engine. I was being repaired part by part as I spent moments praying, worshiping, and supplicating.

At the end of five weeks of treatment, I could walk independently without the wheelchair and the assistance of others. I returned to work after the eighth treatment but with a one-day-a-week treatment and mild painkillers. My spine was repaired, and my spiritual engine was revved after gradually releasing the bitterness. Soon, I could drive out of my "pit stop" renewed and refreshed in the Spirit.

In our experiences in life, God sends help at the right time when He knows we are at the edge of the cliff. The darkest hour may seem very dismal, and the way seems endless, but God will send persons who can identify with our challenges to help lift our spirits. Brother Newton Kelly and Sis Eartha Smith were towers of strength in my darkest hours. Brother Kelly visited and prayed with me and brought books and stories of comfort to read. *The Incredible Power of Prayer* was one book that gave me added strength in my time of pain and suffering. He also gave me a printed copy of the story "Elijah and the Brook." This was quite an interesting story as I saw God's hand in the life of Elijah as God taught Him appropriate lessons. I was taught the lessons of faith and forgiveness through my illness. Sister Smith took me to each of my doctors' appointments. When I offered her money for gas, she turned to me and asked, "Did I ask you for any money? Please put your money back in your purse."

God sent a personal pit crew to care for me as I waited in the pit for healing. Others sent encouragement in songs and speeches. My daughter cried, prayed with, and accompanied me to the doctor whenever I had appointments. She was taught how to lift me from the bed and the chair. She was my main attendant supporting and encouraging me.

It took me six months of agonizing pain, sorrow, and intense reflection and repentance to heal me completely. It took months of doubt, fear, insecurities, unforgiveness, and impatience to realize God's message. Each year, there was some form of unexpected circumstance that would hit harder than a rock, bringing me to my knees. These situations helped me discover how God wants us to stay connected to Him and how He pauses us to repair and service us in His pit stop. This is where we learn good habits that help us maintain the pattern of faith and strengthen us to persevere and find victory in Christ.

The main lesson from my illness, where spiritual growth is concerned, is that forgiveness of our fellow men is essential as it allows us to be forgiven by God for our sins. Additionally, I learned that many times, God stops us in our tracks and immobilizes us so that He can repair us to continue life's journey. Waiting in my "pit stop" for God to fix my broken parts saved my soul.

Meet Evett James

Ms. Evett James Sweeney's passion for counselling led her to pursue her BA in Guidance and Counselling from the Jamaica Theological Seminary. She has acquired other certificates in pre- and post-diagnosis counselling for HIV patients over time. She is a social worker at the Bustamante Hospital for Children, where she is part of the Oncology unit, providing counselling support for cancer patients and their families.

She is the author of ***Encouragement: A Source of Strength for Life's Journey*** and ***Inspirational Healing: A Balm for Healing Souls***. Ms. James Sweeney is also a lover of the arts; she sings, draws, pens poems and short plays, tells stories, and uses these media to empower others to uplift their self-worth.

CHAPTER 13

The Bitter Experiences in my Marital Pit

"For I know the plans I have for you," declares the Lord, "plans to prosper and not to harm you, plans to give you hope and a future." **(Jeremiah 29: 11)**

I had been married for approximately eleven years. Two young children were among the many joys to show. I had fought to build myself for the benefit of my family, and going back to school at night while working in the daytime was one of the sacrifices I made during the process. The journey was challenging, but I fought through teachers' college and university for years. Finally, I was ready to reap the benefits of my hard labour to better our lives and lighten my husband's financial load throughout the journey. I intended to make my family and others more comfortable and happier, especially my husband, who took care of all the family's responsibilities while I was studying. I anticipated spending more time with them and getting a more reasonable salary to improve our lives financially.

Then came the bombshell that shattered my heart completely. "I want a divorce. I will take Martin. You can take Julie." The explosion shook my entire being like a nuclear bomb. I fought to maintain my composure, but internally I was shattered into micro pieces. A million thoughts ricocheted through my mind. Lamentingly, I mulled, *how could this happen? When did we get here? Did I leave too much for him to do? Did I spend too much time on schoolwork, the job, and helping others while neglecting his needs? Is this what pushed him into the arms of another? Was I too busy and preoccupied to see?*

Suddenly he broke the thick, painful silence. "It will be ok; she makes me happy."

I did not cry externally, at least not then, and not for him to see. I reluctantly replied, "Ok, fine, if that is what you want."

Many may wonder why I conceded so quickly. I hoped my response would have given him pause and inspired him to change his mind immediately. I was in a daze. This could not be my reality.

As the days passed, reality hit more and more. Craig started coming home from work later each night, and sometimes he didn't bother to come home. When he was home, he'd lie in bed beside me, talking and laughing for hours on the phone with his sweetheart, while I suffered invisible next to him, weeping and agonizing.

When the pain overwhelmed me, I often left the room to lament to God on the living room floor. He, too, felt very far away. After all, I had also allowed my busy schedule to create a chasm between us. Now, He was all I had to bare my troubled soul. The nights became endless. Sleep was an anomaly, and my husband became colder and more senseless. He was like a stranger living in our house. The once immaculately clean man had stopped showering when he got home. All he did was spend time on the phone with his 'lover.' The kids no longer mattered, and he no longer contributed to paying the bills or helping around the home. He was lost in 'la-la land.'

The days lingeringly and painstakingly drifted into weeks and months, and I grew sick. By then, I had little money to spend, and there was little food for the kids. There were limited funds to care for their school expenses, and the landlord was at my heels, not to mention the mounting medical bills. Increasing hypertension, dizzy spells, countless tests, medications, and doctor visits compounded the tumult. The loss of appetite and the weekly ten pounds weight loss was also much to contend with as I grew weak and listless. I did not share what I was going through with the doctor as yet. I didn't even know what to do. With each passing day, my husband still didn't seem to care, and seldom was he even there, even when he showed up physically.

The nights of crying on the living room floor continued, and I could not understand how we got to this minefield. I didn't even know how to pray. All I could do at times was call out Jesus' name. This was the only thing that helped and sometimes gave me a few minutes of rest. I never knew how or when, but sometimes I drifted asleep. The bitter tears had become my Melatonin, which brought me right back to the words of Job when he said, "My face is flushed from weeping. And deep darkness is on my eyelids." (Job 16:16 NKJV)

Like Job, God was sustaining me. I didn't realize at the time just how much. I had to learn to balance work and life amidst the storm and chaos that ensued. I knew no matter what, I had to be strong for my students. They needed to be taught, nurtured, and loved. I couldn't allow my personal trauma to interfere with and compromise what would be ideal for them.

Amid my turmoil, God provided a tower of strength through sweet Carmella to unload and share the experiences without fear of judgment. Her presence gave me a reason to go on. I dreaded going home to the heart-wrenching experiences each day and not knowing what to expect. God had brought her into my life approximately nine years prior when we both went to interview for the job. God aligned our path and brought her into my life for such a time as this.

As we spoke one afternoon, Carmella recounted the time God carried me through another painful situation. It was a sports day at school and the time for the teachers' race. After much cajoling from my students, I tied my bifocal glasses to my face and lined up for the race. As the race progressed, I began to pull out of last place. Hearing the cheers from my much-excited students, "Run Miss! Run! You can do this! Run Miss, run!" gave me an adrenaline rush to push even harder, and just as suddenly as the bombshell I got from my husband, something struck me. I collided with another teacher and fell face down on the rugged concrete asphalt, shattering my glasses and suffering a hard blow to my head. The silence was so thick it could be cut with a sharp, hot knife. Then came the crying and chaos. I was quickly rushed to the hospital, where I received seven stitches to the forehead and walked away with a fractured right arm, muscle damage to the right foot, and cuts and bruises all over my body.

I remembered contracting chicken pox the following week. I suddenly remembered how cold my husband was. He glared at me in utter disgust and frustration and was seldom there throughout the many doctor and hospital visits. It suddenly dawned on me that I was losing him for a while but was too blind and preoccupied to see. Still, I tried hard to focus on the lesson Carmella was trying to bring home—God had brought me out of that experience, and He would get me through this too.

God provided another friendship for me through Sandra, another coworker who prayed with me in our regular morning and lunchtime prayer sessions. One day, Sandra sent a student to call me. "The adversary wants you dead," she said. "God is fighting for you… your husband is not like his usual self," she continued. "Never stop praying, living for God, and caring for and showing love and compassion to your husband. Love will break the chains and trample the adversary's plot. When you see him act negatively and say horrible things, it's not him; it's the adversary. He loves you, but he is trapped." I tried my best to understand and obey, though, at times, it felt almost impossible. I kept praying for strength to hold on and to break the chains that sought to entrap and destroy my family. I learned to pray more earnestly and relentlessly and trust God above my limited understanding.

On one of my then frequent doctor's visits, my doctor asked me what was going on in my life that was causing my blood pressure to escalate, with persistent dizzy spells and weight loss, even though the medical tests came back negative. He was so kind and even offered financial assistance toward my medical expenses. I felt helpless, so I confided what was happening with my husband. He encouraged me to "spice up" our relationship. "Men love to be charmed and enticed," he said. I contemplated this and convinced myself to get an attractive two-piece lingerie to add to my collection and attempt to rekindle the passion.

One evening when Craig got home from work, I decided to "model" for him, hoping to catch his attention, as my doctor advised. To my great bewilderment, he was distracted, in his world, laughing away on the phone in deep conversation with the one he claimed to love. My heart shattered yet again. I flaunted across the room enticingly, calling out his name. I didn't seem to exist to him. I repeated his name, and this time, he looked up in utter disdain. I pleaded with him and recounted everything I was doing singlehandedly, and he responded, "A dead yuh fi dead!" His voice was different, piercing my heart and soul like a two-edged sword. It sounded like a demon, and his eyes reflected his tone: red, evil, bitter, and cold. I shivered in pain and anger, and suddenly I was enraged. I snatched the phone from his grasp and shattered it on the floor.

The following morning, I mustered up the strength and went to work. I was consumed with regret. I should never have allowed my anger to get the best of me. Still, a part of me felt justified. With bitter tears, I lamented to God and wept.

While at work, I got a message from my school office that there was a missed call from the police station for me. I wondered what it was. The revelation was an even more devastating surprise. My husband had lodged a complaint that I had destroyed the property of the company he was working with; yes, it was the shattered phone. I was warned to replace it, or I would be charged. Tears streamed down my face; tears I thought I had no more of. Carmella was there to dry them, encourage me and pray, while the greatest Friend I could ever have interceded for me in the Most Holy of the sanctuary. He had provided this earthly friend to do as close as humanly possible for me. This was another way in which He carried me through my marital pit. "My intercessor is my friend as my eyes pour out tears to God; on behalf of a man he pleads with God as one pleads for a friend." (Job 16: 20-21 NIV)

Life started becoming more and more of a dreadful nightmare for me. At times I felt numb, and other times I thought I couldn't go on. Somehow my precious little angels, Martin and Julian, would see the tears I tried so hard to conceal. They were so young and innocent. It could destroy them, still many times they were the ones who brought comfort and reassurance. With what seemed loving concerns beyond their years, they gently hugged and kissed me while saying, "We love you, Mommy. Everything will be ok. Jesus will fix it all for us." These were some of the things that kept me going. Occasionally, Sandra called and prayed with me and encouraged me to keep caring for my husband and never stop praying for and loving him. "Be kind and compassionate to one another, forgiving each other, just as in Christ God forgave you." (Ephesians 4:32). Sometimes this felt hard and impossible to do, but God kept me.

At times I felt Craig didn't deserve my love, care, and forgiveness. *He is too wicked,* I thought. Other times I thought, *who am I not to*

The Bitter Experiences in my Marital Pit

forgive when I being so dreadful and sinful, so wretched and terrible, need forgiveness too?

The time went by, and things only changed for the worse. Craig came home whenever he felt, and without showering, he went to bed and eagerly picked up his phone to communicate with his 'lover.' His bowel movements seemed more and more frequent. He cared nothing about the care and upkeep of the home, and his personal hygiene was on the decline.

It was the Easter holiday, and I was preparing to attend church with the kids on the Sabbath morning. Craig said he was going to work but wanted me to take the kids to the country and spend the holiday with his relatives there. I didn't like the idea, and all that plagued my mind was the thought that he wanted the time and freedom to spend with his 'lover,' even to take her to the house. I hardly thought I was paranoid, and he was adamant that I go. Instead, I took the children to church without his knowledge.

The day was well spent in the presence of the Lord, and worship took all the worries and cares off my mind. However, after church, I started feeling uneasy. I felt the sudden urge to leave but not to go home, especially since I saw myriad of missed calls and messages on my phone from him insisting that we go to the country. I eventually took the kids and went by my sister's house. While there, I heard heavy, persistent knocks on the grill and loud tones of Craig insisting on seeing me and the kids. I made sure not to go out there and kept the kids locked in the bedroom. Craig stayed there for quite some time, complaining, and whining to my sister, who wasn't intrigued to listen. He eventually left.

Waiting In the Pit

I began my journey early the following day to Carmella's home, where I sought refuge. Craig kept calling and messaging, and of course, I ignored them. I didn't know what to expect from him; after all, he was armed (though legally), and he had begun to feel like nothing short of a monster to me. Sunday night, I got a call from his aunt saying that her nephew had said I took his kids and ran away. He did not say where I was going, and I wasn't responding to his calls and messages. At this point, the aunt was aware of some of our challenges but was oblivious to the excruciating details. I did not want to get the extended family involved, so I gave her a brief synopsis of what was transpiring and asked her to pray for us.

Later that night, I got a call from my sister. She related a message from her landlord, who had seen me only once. The message was pretty much the same as Sandra's. "Your sister's husband is with another woman by which he is captivated, but he still loves his wife. Whatever he does and says, it's not him; the spell just blinds him. Tell her never to stop praying for and loving her husband." She went as far as outlining the changes in Craig's behavior.

"He ate something from the girl," she said. "She would have noticed him going to the bathroom frequently, and when he talks to her, it's like it's not his voice at times." My sister was shivering in disbelief as she relayed the message. Her landlord did not know me this way, and neither did she know my husband. She also didn't know Sandra, who had related the same message to me. I realized that it must have been the voice of the Lord speaking through them to save me and my family. The last statement was what gave me the greatest comfort. "I am praying for her, and God will fix it as long as she keeps trusting Him and obey." I prayed and went to bed.

I went back home with mixed emotions. I still did not know what to expect, but I knew God was protecting me, so I wasn't as fearful as before. I was reminded of the text, "For God has not given us the spirit of fear, but of power and of love and of a sound mind." (2 Timothy 1:7 NKJV)

Craig said nothing to me when I got home, and I decided to start sleeping in the children's room. I decided that, like fearlessness, wisdom is also pivotal. "The one who gets wisdom loves life; the one who cherishes understanding will soon prosper" (Proverbs 19:8 NIV)

I woke up the Wednesday morning out of food and medication and the landlord on my tail for the rent. My savings were depleted. My salary had gone significantly low with paying back loans for school, taking care of my dad and other expenses. I did not know what to do. As I lay in the bed, I suddenly mustered up the strength to cry to my heavenly Father, *"God, please help me. I do not have anyone else to turn to."* I heard the soft, gentle voice of the Holy Spirit say, *"Go to the JTA."* The JTA is my Credit Union from which I had gotten my previous loans for school fees and other expenditures. As far as I was concerned, I could not get any other loans, nor did I have the take-home salary to cushion it, so I hesitated. The voice of the Lord persisted until I could do nothing but obey.

Waiting In the Pit

Reluctantly, I got up from the bed, got dressed, and started my journey to the JTA. Again, I heard the soft, still voice of the Lord saying, *"Don't worry, my child; I will take care of it for you."*

As I arrived at the JTA office, I saw a coworker who told me how she had applied for and got her visa for the United States. She asked me why I didn't apply for mine too. Little did I know what the Lord was doing. As I sat before the loan representative, I felt compelled to relate what had happened to me at school when I fell while running the teachers' race. I told them of my medical bills and what I was going through health-wise.

"You do not know if the fall and hitting your head on the asphalt is causing these things to happen to you," she said. "Please give me a few minutes."

I soon discovered that the sales representative was speaking to the manager who had written a big cheque. It was enough to cover my medical expenses, pay off my rent, get groceries for my house and my dad, have excess to make my visa application, as my coworker previously recommended, and more. "What a God!" is all I could have proclaimed. Glory be to the Lord God Almighty. "But my God shall supply all your needs according to His riches in glory by Jesus Christ." (Philippians 4:19)

I had a prayer and fasting session that day, so I journeyed there after leaving the JTA. I sat in church and reflected on the goodness of God, knowing that He is always taking care of me, come what may. All I needed to do was to trust Him and obey. While in prayerful reflection, I felt the minister come before me. He suddenly dressed back and said, "Oh Lord have mercy, you are going through so much, but your heart is so loving and kind. Have you ever traveled before?" He continued, "I see papers, and I also see the number 19. You will travel, and when you come back, things will be different."

The minister prayed for me and my family there and then. I thought about how my coworker recommended that I apply before I got the money, and now the minister mentioned the visa again. I called and made an appointment with the travel agent. This was the beginning of what seemed to be a God-sent aligned mystery and a marvelous miracle that was played out at just the right time.

My pit was dark, cold, and miserable. I often thought I would drown and suffocate from the grime in the pit of my marriage, but God had a marvelous plan only He could contrive. While waiting in your pit of darkness and gloom, God is busy orchestrating and planning the date and every detail of your deliverance. Anticipate the move. Anticipate the miracle.

CHAPTER 13.5

The Ticket out of my Pit

"The Lord works in mysterious ways, His wonders to perform." ***(Luke 24:16)***

(Continues from Chapter 13)

Waiting for a reprieve in a pit of marital turbulence is one of the most daunting experiences I have ever had. Living with the man I had committed to love a little over a decade prior, for better or worse, and watching him transform into the worst monster as my emotional, mental, and physical health declined, was becoming unbearable. The Lord knew I needed deliverance, or else I would shatter into unmendable pieces like my glasses when I fell on the concrete asphalt that sad day. He had a plan. I had to wait, trust and believe.

The date came for my US Visa appointment. At the US Embassy, I watched individuals being turned down by a particular interviewer. I prayed I wouldn't end up going to him. It then came

The Ticket out of my Pit

home to me; right there on my paper was number 19. In the interviewer's section, the number 19 was also plastered there. As I reflected on what the minister said, I felt the fear and anxiety slowly drifting away, and I started thanking God for what He had in store. As I walked confidently to be interviewed by the gentleman at window 19, I knew God already had it covered. The interviewer asked me only two questions, and yes, the ten years visa was granted. "Oh God, You are indeed an amazing God!" I proclaimed. "Thank You for all that You do. Surely, Lord, Your words are true and just."

One afternoon after work, I decided to visit my dad and take groceries for him. I conversed, worshipped with him, then went home. Upon reaching home, I went into our matrimonial bedroom to put my bag down. Immediately, I heard the voice of the Holy Spirit saying, *"Kneel and pray for your husband."* I hesitated but then yielded to His plea as it came home more forcefully and profoundly. *"Kneel and pray for your husband."* The Holy Spirit inspired what to say: *"Lord, I glorify Your name for being a merciful, loving, and forgiving God. As I kneel to pray to You, I ask that You forgive me of my sins. I place my husband before You right now, Jesus. Please forgive him as well. Please deliver him from the adversary's trap. Protect and keep him in Your loving care and grant him another chance to surrender his all to You. Please break the chains and set Your son free. Thank you for hearing and answering my heart's cry; I pray. Amen."*

As I arose, I wondered why I was suddenly prompted to pray for my husband. I reflected on the incredible and supportive husband, father, and person he was before I started coming home to this "demonic stranger" in our house. As I greeted and spoke with our

Waiting In the Pit

children, the voice came back to me, *"Kneel and pray for your husband."* I did, yet again. I wrestled with the Holy Spirit in deep lamentations. I begged the Lord to put a shield around him, snatch him back from the ultimate enemy of his soul, heal, cleanse, and make him whole, and have mercy on him and set him free. As I got deeper and deeper into prayer, I heard my cell phone ringing. The Holy Spirit prompted me not to stop praying. As I continued, the phone kept ringing until it eventually stopped.

After praying, I checked my phone and realized Craig had been calling. My heart was increasingly softening and anxious, so I called back but only got his voicemail. *I hope he is ok.* As I sat to talk with the children about their day, the phone rang again. It was Craig. I answered eagerly. He recounted what happened when he was first calling. "I was on a Hiace bus traveling back from the country," he said. "While on the highway, I heard a loud explosion. It was the sound of the bursting of the rear tire on the side of the bus that I was sitting on. This threw the bus over to the side where I was sitting. Then, I reached for my phone and tried to call you, but it fell from my hand and fell open during the process. Though the bus was on its side, I could see and feel it speeding down the highway, ready to explode in the concrete barrier to the side. I was certain I would die at this time, but something amazing happened. As the bus approached the concrete wall, I closed my eyes and said, 'This is it!' But the bus stopped abruptly, only inches away from the concrete wall. This was nothing short of a miracle, especially with the speed at which it was coming down the highway. I had to find the pieces to my phone to put it back together and call you back," he said.

The Ticket out of my Pit

Deep within my heart, I began to praise and thank God. God prompted me to pray for my husband at the right time. I thought of His unconditional love. I thought of His mercy and His forgiving power. Oh, the wonderful promises of His Word, that always stand true. "He shall call upon Me, and I will answer him: I will be with him in trouble; I will deliver him and honour him." (Psalm 91:15)

As all this was taking over my mind, I heard Craig say, "I'm at the Spanish Town Hospital. Are you coming?"

Right there and then, an inner voice spoke, *why does he want me to come? Why doesn't he call his girl? I didn't know where he was coming from; now I must leave for the hospital.* I knew this wasn't the calm, sweet, forgiving voice that prompted me to pray before.

I then heard another voice that was soft, sweet, and gentle, *"Yes, my child, go and take care of your husband. This is Him."* I thought this was my loving, forgiving God. I said to Craig, "Yes, of course, I am coming, baby," and I did. What a difference it makes to know, listen, and obey the voice of the Lord. "My sheep hear my voice, and I know them, and they follow me." (John 10: 27)

At the hospital, Craig was quite a grouch. The skin from his back and left shoulder were badly peeled from its contact with the highway road as the bus skidded with him. His shirt had to be cut from his body. He had to remain shirtless because of his injuries and was cold and in excruciating pain. He shivered as he waited for tests to be done. The painkillers he was given seemed to make little or no difference. As he murmured and complained, I started to think why I was the one there, but I fought to do what I thought was right and what the Lord wanted me to do, especially when I thought of how different that accident could have turned out.

Craig was discharged from the hospital in the wee hour of the morning. That was the first time I slept with my husband in our marital bed in months. As I hugged and comforted him, I thanked the Lord again for sparing his life and being such an extraordinary God.

In the morning, there were legal matters to take care of at the police station. I stayed home with Craig, prepared his breakfast, accompanied him to the police station, and did everything he needed. Carmella, my best friend, was hurt. She didn't think that her friend, who had been through so much, should be the one waiting on such a "cruel man," hand and foot. She thought the other girl should have been doing this. She was so hurt for her friend and reasonably so. She knew the excruciating pains and experiences I had gone through. After all, she was the one there to cry the bitter tears with and was the shoulders I leaned on and the ears to listen. She could not understand why I could be so "stupid" to be doing all I was now doing for him. Carmella's pain was compounded as the days passed, and I no longer had time to talk. I was busy hustling home immediately after work each day to care for Craig.

The routine continued for months, and it was nearing our wedding anniversary. I had not stopped caring for Craig, but things still felt wrong. Finally, it was February 14th, the day of our anniversary, and Craig said nothing to me that morning. As I got ready for work, I hoped with everything in my heart that he would remember. It was Valentine's Day, the day the world celebrated as

The Ticket out of my Pit

the day of love, which should make it a lot easier to remember. As I left for work, he still said nothing, and I went with the pain shattering my heart and tears engulfing my face, just as they did before the accident. As I pushed myself to walk to the bus stop, I wondered, like a zombie, *is this girl still in my husband's life? What had happened since the accident?* As far as I know, he had been home this entire time, and I cared for him.

I didn't know how I made it through the day, but I did. I had to watch as Carmella gave me a passing wave from upstairs and a distant look that gnawed on the preexisting pains of my broken heart. Was *Carmella's feeling that I was being foolish and that I was allowing Craig to use me justified?* When I got home, things were pretty much the same. As I lay beside Craig, all sorts of thoughts engulfed my mind. The only difference was that he wasn't on the phone with the girl this time. I did not even know when I fell asleep after praying.

Early the following day, I awoke to get ready for work. Opening my eyes, I noticed Craig's phone was not under his pillow. He had been sleeping with it under there all this time, which meant he had something to hide. As I froze, staring at the phone, I felt compelled to take it up and see if I could find the answers to some of my questions. I was torn between taking and leaving it. Eventually, I gave in to the temptation and took it up. As I went into the bathroom to go through it, I locked the door so Craig wouldn't wake up and find me. As I went through the call log, there were many calls between them daily. I then went into the messages and saw him outlining how much he loved and missed her, telling her "Happy Valentine's Day," and expressing how

Waiting In the Pit

beautiful she looked with her new hairstyle. She responded, "You would love me just the same, even without my hair done." I started shivering, and my hands began shaking as I fought to hold back the screams and the tears streaming down my face.

I wept bitterly and heard a loud banging on the bathroom door. It was Craig with the monstrous voice again, "Where is my phone?" He shouted. I did not answer. I had no voice left. The banging increased and became more vicious and invasive. "Open the door and give me back my phone!" I kept on searching. I needed to know exactly what it was, and I could not open the door with him in that rage.

Craig hissed his teeth and boisterously said, "All the same, I don't care. See what you want to see!" When I left the bathroom to go to the room, he was sitting at the edge of the bed, looking at me in what seemed to be a brief moment of compassion, quickly replaced by the familiar evil, glaring look from bloody-looking eyes. He shouted, "A that yuh fi get! Mi nuh know weh yuh tek up mi phone fah!" The tone in his voice and the demonic glare were pretty much the same as the ones I experienced that night he said I should die. I gave him his phone as I fought to hold back the tears. I was sure I saw another look of compassion in his eyes, again quickly engulfed by the bitter, evil look of hatred. I left and was forced hard to muster up the strength to go to work. All I could whisper was, "Jesus, please help me again."

While at work that day, Sandra called me to pray. She shared the Word of God, reminding me that God would never give us more than we can bear, that He would never leave nor forsake us, and He would always take care of His own. "The Lord himself goes before you and will be with you; he will never leave nor forsake you. Do not be afraid; do not be discouraged." (Deuteronomy 31:8 NIV). I gathered the strength to go on. As the days went by, I found more strength in the Word and the tender little hugs and kisses of my precious children. At church, I was transported to a place of solitude and peace as I worshipped and lifted songs of praise to my God. I even found the strength to fast and pray, which helped. This kept me grounded and stronger with each passing day. All this time, I never stopped taking care of my husband with tender, loving care, though, at times, I felt like I shouldn't. It was as though nothing had happened on Craig's part, and I never spoke about the incident but went on day by day with God's strength.

It was fast approaching the Easter holiday again, and I got a call of concern from my eldest sister abroad. She wanted to know how I was doing, as she felt something was wrong. She had heard from my other sister that I had persistent medical issues. She found out I was not well and wanted to give me a vacation so I could relax and destress, though she had no idea of the magnitude of what I was going through. I reflected on what the minister had said about my visa, which I had gotten. I also recalled his prophecy of how I would travel and how things would be different when I returned.

Craig had no idea I had gotten the visa, as I didn't know what to expect from him. I also didn't tell him I was planning to leave the island. I was only forced to do so a few days before I left because of the children and the arrangement to have them stay with my sister while I was away, as he had returned to work.

Early in the morning, while I was getting ready to go to the airport, Craig came to me with the compassion in his eyes that was short-lived in previously horrific experiences and said, "So you're leaving now? Take care and enjoy yourself." I hugged him and said thank you. At that moment, I felt things had already begun to change, even as I left. While abroad, I took the time to get even closer to God. The vacation time spent with my sister, brother-in-law, nieces, and newfound friends helped to soothe the wounds that still lingered, but still, I missed my children and husband dearly. To my surprise, Craig called at times to check up on me. When I called my sister with whom my children were staying, I learned that he had been making regular visits there to take things for them and ensure they were ok. I thanked God for the seeming breakthroughs each day and never ceased to pray. "Rejoice always, pray without ceasing, give thanks in all circumstances; for this is the will of God in Christ Jesus for you." (1 Thessalonians 5: 16-17 NKJV)

It was soon time for me to return home. I would have had a great time with my extended family members hadn't my heart been elsewhere. They understood the sadness that I endured, though they could never fathom all I would have been through as I never entirely divulged. The flight was pleasant, the reunion joyful, as I hugged and kissed the sweet babies I missed dearly, and there he was. Craig welcomed me back home with a big, lingering hug when he got home from work. As we lay in bed that night, he turned and said, "Dear, do you remember when you asked that we see a family counselor together? If you still want us to, we can." I felt the positive transformation deep within my heart. As the days went by, I started to know him again in every sense of the word. The loving, hard-working, ambitious, immaculate gentleman that I had gotten married to. I don't remember strictly and entirely how and when it happened, but I know it could only be God. I prayed each day that He would completely save my husband's soul and make him whole. "You intended to harm me, but God intended it for good to accomplish what is now being done, the saving of many lives." (Genesis 50:20 NIV)

Approximately twelve years after the varying experiences mentioned of being in the pit, I inevitably reflect on how far God has elevated me and my immediate family. I am constantly reminded of God's goodness and grace in this life's journey. All glory be to His high and holy name.

The relationship between my husband and myself is better than before. We now share a union of twenty-two years, with better communication and appreciation for each other. I was initially reluctant to share with him the horrific experiences of all that transpired during what I call the season of "demon possession." When I eventually did, which was recent, he was oblivious to all that transpired. I can't adequately explain but I know God delivered him. "I sought the Lord, and He heard me, and delivered me from all my fears." (Psalm 34:4)

The deliverance came in so many wonderful, miraculous ways that words are inadequate to fully express and encapsulate the gratitude pouring from our hearts to God. He blessed us with a beautiful three-bedroom house during this pit experience. The address also includes the number 19 that the minister saw, the same number on my visa application. Acquiring this home was another marvel as we moved in before paying a dime. What an amazing God!

Our children are now grown. Our daughter graduated from law school with first-class honours and other awards and scholarships. She also completed Norman Manley Law School after receiving various scholarships and awards, including Top Student of the Year. Our son is presently studying with dreams of becoming a cardiothoracic surgeon.

We have concluded that, like Joseph, sometimes our pit experiences are used as steppingstones to fulfill God's purpose in our lives and to bless others along the way. "Count it all joy, my brothers, when you meet trials of various kinds, for you know that the testing of your faith produces steadfastness. And let steadfastness have its full effect, that you may be perfect and complete, lacking in nothing." (James 1:2-4 ESV)

Meet Stephanie Minto-Hinds

Stephanie Minto-Hinds has been a devoted Christian for almost her entire life. She has experienced mighty miracles at the hand of God after having gone through extenuating circumstances and experiences.

Stephanie has been a teacher for over twenty years and holds a Bachelor of Arts in Education and Literacy and a tentative Master's Degree in Curriculum Development.

Stephanie has been married for over twenty years and has proven that you can navigate any aspect of your life with God, unconditional love, and forgiveness. She is the proud mother of two adult children; and an aspiring lawyer and cardiothoracic surgeon.

CHAPTER 14

Restored in the Pit

"And I will restore to you the years that the locust hath eaten, the cankerworm, and the caterpillar, and the palmerworm, my great army which I sent among you."
(Joel 2:25)

The heart-rending memories of crying and screaming relentlessly as I fought to get on the bus with my mother so that she wouldn't leave me again while my dad struggled to restrain me are not as vivid as they used to be. I was eight months old when my mom and I were separated. It was not a decision she made willingly, but one she had to agree with out of respect and obedience to her mother. My mother gave birth to me at eighteen, and her mother thought it was wise to relocate her to a more civilized part of Jamaica to pursue a promising career and advance herself. I was left in the care of my grandmother and father, who took excellent care of me; but they were not my mother.

Dad was present daily, and each morning, he took me for a walk before I went to school and walked me back home in the evenings.

I slept with my grandma nightly as I was fearful of her being taken away as well while I slept. Occasionally, my mom came to visit, and whenever it was time for her to leave, my heart collapsed with sorrow. I was inconsolable, and it took me days to recuperate. The sadness in her eyes told me that she, too, was brokenhearted, but she had to go, and this continued until I was eight years old.

Although I had my grandmother and dad, I yearned for my mother's tender love and care. Every little girl had their mother, but I didn't. Every Sunday, I wished my mom was at church to see me adorned in the pearls, heels, and beautiful dresses she bought me and to hear me quoting the golden text, St. John 3:16, which I was tasked to read on Sunday mornings. I was a cheerful and promising child who loved school, church, and home. My academic performance was superb, and my teachers loved me.

One day, my grandmother decided to send me away to live with my mother because of my academic success. She thought living in the city would be better for me and yield great results and opportunities. I was happy to live with my mother but also sad that I had to leave my family. They were all I had and knew, but Grandma's decision was final. Dad was not happy. However, he complied. I was going to miss my family, but a part of me was ready to leave the environment that was becoming unsafe and unhealthy.

A relative was verbally abusing me, and a neighbor was molesting me. I wanted to escape it all. My guardians didn't know about the molestation; however, they were aware of my relative's verbal abuse and intervened, but she did not cooperate. Weeks passed, and it was now time to bid my farewell. It was a bittersweet moment that lived with me for years and gave me anxiety attacks whenever I thought about it.

When I finally arrived at my new home, I felt in my gut that things were about to change drastically. I was in unfamiliar territory with new people who were blood-related but were foreign to me. I soon discovered that my mom was living with them, and that was where I would reside too. This was not what my grandmother told me, so I wondered, *was grandma tired of me and lied that I would live with my mother. Why didn't my father stop her?* From that moment, I started thinking something was wrong with me, and nobody wanted me. I began to feel unloved, abandoned, rejected, guilty, and insecure. Getting acquainted with my cousins didn't take a long time, but I did not feel like I belonged in their home. My mother was unhappy but didn't make it noticeable. She was sent away for a better life, but instead, she became a house aid to her sister, catering to the entire family, which made her feel unfulfilled. We did not bond like we should, given how stressed, uncertain about her future, used, frustrated, and broken she was. My cousins and I only bonded during playtime, making me feel insecure, abandoned, and unloved.

I was enrolled in school and placed in second grade among the top performers, but soon, my academic performance was below average. I was becoming depressed and had a challenging time grasping my lessons. I was battling with all those feelings, and the kids at my new school started accusing me of stealing money. I missed my family and friends and desperately wanted to return to the country, but that would never happen. So, I eagerly anticipated holidays to visit them.

One day, my aunt, who I was living with, announced that they were moving to a more civilized neighborhood, and sadly, I had to move with them. My mom went to stay with a friend who was like her sister, but it wasn't convenient for me to go with her, so I was stuck with the family, which made me feel like an intruder. I wondered if this would be the story of my life: separation, instability, and breaking bonds with loved ones. Absolutely nothing felt right about this.

My cousins and I started a new school, and it didn't take long before my teacher noticed something was wrong with me. She thought I was struggling with personal issues and believed I would be more productive if they were resolved. *Something was wrong, but how was I supposed to tell her what it was? I was afraid to tell her I didn't feel loved, liked, or wanted. I couldn't tell her that my mother didn't want me. I would not dare have anyone think badly of my family, especially my mother. It hurts that I could not express how I felt.* I internalized it all.

One day, Mom came by the house and told me I would now live with her, and I was happy. *Maybe we could create a mother-daughter bond now that we were living together and by ourselves*, I thought. But that didn't happen as I supposed it would.

I was re-enrolled into the primary school I attended prior because it was close to where she lived. Soon, it was time for another transition to a bigger house, as my mom wanted me to have my own space. We spent little time bonding, and I felt like something was missing. However, I paid little attention because I had playmates and many toys. *What more could a little girl my age ask for? At least I was living with her.* I was happy.

Little did I know that a familiar monster lurked in the shadows, waiting to pounce upon me again. A child molester lived next door to our apartment, and I was already his target. Soon, I fell into his net. The sorrowful memories of my encounters with my neighbor in the country flooded my mind and gave me anxiety attacks. His friend also started touching me inappropriately. I had to tell Mom, but she found it hard to believe because many people respected my neighbor.

This worked in the man's favor as his pedophilic disorder intensified, and he continued feeding his fetish. I was ashamed, fearful, and overwhelmed by the recurrence of this traumatic experience. The feelings of being bound, helpless, powerless, and guilty stifled and choked me constantly. No one believed that these grown men were obsessed with my little body. Their stares nauseated me and caused me to shiver in fear. I was angry and frustrated, and I hated my body.

Things worsened, as I was accused of stealing money and dinnerware from the cabinet. I was also labeled promiscuous and accused of going to a man's house after school. I never had a boyfriend and had no interest in any. I wanted to enjoy my childhood, but it was already tainted. Things in my home got terrible as my mom was always upset, and I didn't know why. My depression worsened, and I was failing my classes as it became challenging to concentrate. I lost interest in everything, but I kept going to church. It was the only place I found solace. I was at church every Sunday, during weekdays, and on trips to visit other church events. As I matured, I realized that nothing else mattered but to be in a place where I could find peace, and being around individuals who loved God was a joy to my soul.

Sometimes at home, I cried until I had panic attacks. I was scared and tormented and wished I was anything but human. I wanted to escape the pain of my life. Somedays, the thought of never returning home from school engulfed my mind. I wanted to escape my current situation, but I thought my mother would be devastated if I ever went missing. For some strange reason, I knew she loved me but was battling her insecurities and fears and felt hopeless. Having those thoughts was what helped me to love her during those traumatic moments. God must have given me a different heart.

It seemed there was no chance of us ever getting to know each other as everything was happening and changing so fast. What was supposed to be a place of safety felt like a time bomb waiting to explode. I couldn't understand why my mother was genuinely nice to everyone else but dealt with me harshly and with resentment and anger. I felt like a supernatural force was coming between us, but I didn't understand spiritual warfare. It all continued until the brutal announcement that I was expecting a child. The news spread like wildfire. My cousins knew I had no boyfriend before my pregnancy, so they were shocked and had questions.

One Friday afternoon on June 25, 1999, while on my way from school, I detoured to a home where my mom's coworker lived with her son. He had become my first boyfriend after visiting the house to get my hair done, which led to an impulsive intimate encounter. The entanglement started with the fear of him leaving and was compounded by guilt, shame, and disappointment.

I tried to deepen my relationship with the Lord to escape something I knew could ruin my life, but I felt trapped. He expected my visits to his home, and I thought I had to oblige because I feared he would tell his mother of our first encounter then my mother would hear and finish me. I got caught in a web and had no idea how to escape. I was mentally disturbed and emotionally unbalanced.

The time to face the impending judgment in my home was fast approaching. All the accusations were deemed accurate because my pregnancy proved that I was sleeping around. Perhaps it was the accusations that lured me into that trap. I also discovered that after my stepdad heard the allegations, he declared teenage pregnancy over my life. The Bible speaks about the power of the tongue.

My mother was angry and disappointed. I was sixteen and pregnant. Given the baby's dad's denial of impregnating me, the burden of all my prenatal care and responsibilities was left for my mother and stepdad to carry. Although he told his mother he had nothing to do with it, he did not deny the claims when asked by his stepdad. I wasn't bold enough to confront him. Instead, I opened my heart to receive what he claimed was love because it felt good to hear someone ask, "Are you ok?" And to say, "I love you." Even though they were words without meaning, they reassured my soul and filled a void I had carried for years.

The hostility continued in my home, day, and night. I cannot recall a moment of peace and tranquility during those nine months of gestation. One morning, I woke up and found my mother in a murderous rage. She hurled every harsh and demeaning word at me. The words sunk deep in my heart like the dog bite I had recently suffered. These words mercilessly and viciously pierced my sore spot. I wanted to die suddenly and even attempted suicide, but that was to get my mother's attention. I needed her comfort as I was an emotional wreck, but instead, her response when she was called to the scene sank deep in my heart and shattered it into a million pieces. I was cold, numb, and speechless; tears were the only language I spoke for days. I was constantly told to leave the house as my presence became unbearable. Everyone in the community knew that not only was I a pregnant teenager, but they also learned about the hostility I was facing in my home, and I was ashamed.

Despite the emotional detachment, my mother's physical support was evident as I lacked nothing from the discovery of my unplanned pregnancy to birth. However, after having my son, I didn't think things could worsen. Everything I did or said was misunderstood, and I couldn't make myself clear. My anguish was deep and dark, and there was no possible sign of light in my situation. By then, I had accepted that my mother hated me. I feared my emotional pain would endanger my son's well-being, and I wanted to escape with him, but I felt helpless.

We moved from that community to another after the woman whose man molested me conspired against us with the homeowners. After we moved, we ended up moving twice again before we finally settled. I gained employment, and this was a new beginning. I started working on my future goals hoping that things would be better, but the possibility of things being better was unlikely to happen; if so, it was no time soon. My accomplishments and efforts in becoming a phenomenal woman after teenage pregnancy were unrecognized. I felt isolated, dejected, and alone.

One night, after trying to state my opinion during a heated argument, I was thrown out of the house with my clothes like Hagar, who was banished to the desert with Ishmael. I had nowhere to go, so I took refuge at a bus stop for a few hours before my stepdad came looking for me.

I thought my mother was losing her mind. She was a total stranger and with each day she got angrier. Sometimes when arguments got heated, I was physically wounded, and although those scars could be seen, I had deeper emotional scars that were not easily seen. Even though no one seemed to care to minister healing to my sore in that deep pit of sorrow, I still masked the pain. I learned to fast, pray, lean, and depend on God in my pit. I thought I had lost everything, but I still believed in God.

It was tough to thrive in that dark and depressive hole, but I found strength in God while waiting for the light to come and for deliverance to overtake me. This continued for years until Mom left Jamaica in 2008. I was afraid I would never see her again and didn't want her to go, but she needed the break.

In August 2011, we reunited for the first time in three years when I visited America on a work and travel program for university students. She was the one who sponsored my trip and paid my tuition fee for the first semester. I was pursuing a bachelor's degree in guidance and counseling, which I was passionate about.

Our reunion was a tearful one. We hugged tightly like we were afraid of being separated again.

She visited Jamaica one month after I returned home, and the minute she entered the yard, it felt like a bomb was about to explode. My sister and I hugged and welcomed her. I wondered *what* was going to happen and *when*. The following morning, while conversating, I was accused of conspiring to rob her to start a business. I had previously sought her assistance, to which she agreed but later denied me the loan. I was petrified, and my breath escaped my lungs for a few seconds. I ran to a neighbor's house and fainted on her floor. The devil was mad that I didn't die from heart failure, and so the following day, he led my mother to humiliate me in the presence of my aunt and cousins who had come to visit her. With hatred and anger, she shouted, "If you think I will file for you to live in America, you've made the saddest mistake." I felt a lump in my throat and almost suffocated from the unseen tears. I was embarrassed, but I knew it was a demonic attack, so I remained speechless.

After she returned to America, I cried for her like I did when she visited me as a child. No matter what happened between us, I yearned for her love and attention, but apparently, she didn't know she was rejecting me.

My son later migrated to the United States at the age of fourteen, and the separation forced me to obtain a visitor's visa so that I could see and spend time with him. I stayed with my mom, but the relationship felt forced. I needed my mother. I finally migrated to the United States in 2018, hoping for a fresh start, but instead, I was constantly in mental turmoil.

In 2020, the Lord impressed upon my heart to travel to another state, and with much confirmation, I pitched my tent, but God had another plan. After He fulfilled His purpose, He ushered me back to my mother's house in precisely six months amid the Covid19 pandemic. In that year, I hoped I would begin to see victory in every area of my life, but one day, the Lord told me that He would fulfill His promises in my fortieth year. That was another three years of waiting, but He gave me the peace and patience to wait. I knew restoring the relationship with mom was a part of that promise. I began to analyze my personal growth and development and sought help in areas I needed to mature. I wanted to be ready for God's next move. It was hard, but I didn't give up because I was intentional. I was getting ready to be lifted from the pit where I was deeply sunk for almost all my life. I later moved to another borough in New York to preserve the peace I had found and pursue some things I longed for, but after three months, circumstances led me right back to my mother. I was not upset, and God had given me the ability to understand that it was not time to move away from my family. My eyes began to open to the devil's devices and how he strategically planned his attacks against my family. And so, my prayers became strategic and were like missiles in his kingdom of darkness. I gained strength that only God could've given me.

I desired complete restoration in my entire household, and I clothed myself in the armor of God and wrestled against the principalities and powers assigned to my home. Some days seemed uncertain, but I held on to the word God gave me in 2020. His appointed time was worth waiting on. He didn't promise that my days would be smooth, but He promised to restore me. He was with me in my pit as he promised never to leave or forsake me.

After almost three decades of living in a dark and cold place filled with sorrow and grief, I began to see the light and feel the warmth of the love I longed for. The place that was once wet and messy from the tears I cried, is now uncluttered and peaceful as God washed away the years of immense pain. God kept me afloat, so the despair, hopelessness, depression, and rejection did not overtake me.

The Word of God says weeping may endure for a night, but joy comes in the morning. There was never a morning. Discovering that God has a strange way of shaking things up in the midnight hour, I started praying in that dark place more than I ever did. I fasted and prayed, worshipped, and praised God in my pit. He was there inhabiting my praises. It was time to mount up, so He gave me wings like an eagle. Little did I know that the mess thrown at my mother and me in our pit would be packaged into a beautiful, life-changing message. God turned our tests into testimonies, trials into triumphs, and brokenness into breakthroughs.

I almost gave up on ever feeling loved by my mother. I no longer tried to prove that my love for her was pure and I had no ill feelings toward her. It was about time that I realized my mother would never see me the way a daughter wants to be seen by her mother, so I was going to give up on that too. I almost gave up on having the peace of God in my home. There is a song, "He's Able," by Deitrick Haddon, and a line that says, "Don't give up on God, 'cause He won't give up on you. He's able."

Today I can testify according to His Word in Ephesians 3:20, "He is able to do exceedingly, abundantly above all that we can ask or think."

In my distress and sometimes feeling of giving up, I grab hold of the horns of the altar. I pleaded my need before God, and He supplied it. I began to walk through our apartment day and night and pray. I anointed the doors and windows and declared the Word of God. I prayed over my mother's pillow, consecrated it, and declared peace to her mind.

I recall having a conversation with her, which led us to tears. I held her and prayed; then I heard something like heavy chains fall to the ground. I stopped and looked, but then I discerned it was not natural chains, so I continued praying. I had to pray for personal deliverance, restoration, and healing of my wounds as well. The chains were broken, and the yokes were destroyed. My family has been healed, delivered, and restored. My mother and I have the best relationship. It's more than I could ask for.

The devil used the separation as an opportunity to try to destroy and pervert my destiny. He blinded my mother's eyes so that she could not see the prized possession that she had given birth to. What he meant for evil, God turned it around for our good.

There is no test you can't pass, tears He won't wipe, and trials you can't overcome. God will cause you to triumph so that you may live to testify how you waited in the pit for His appointed time to be restored.

Meet Nadian "Lady Theresa" Reid

Nadian "Lady Theresa" Reid is the visionary of SuperMother's Strength Ministries. She is an intercessor, mentor, best-selling author, transformational speaker, Christian life coach, philanthropist, and teenage mother advocate.

She is the mother of two amazing and brilliant young men who affectionately calls her "Prayer Momma." Professionally, she is a newborn care specialist and an entrepreneur.

CHAPTER 15

Pit Hopping

"For thou art my hope, O Lord God: Thou art my trust from my youth. By thee have I been holden up from the womb: Thou art he that took me out of my mother's bowels: My praise shall be continually of thee." **(Psalm 71:5-6)**

On October 1, 2021, at 8 am, while traveling to a meeting in the neighboring parish of St. Elizabeth from my hometown in Hanover, Jamaica, I was flung into an agonizing pit that I will possibly reside in for a lifetime (unless God performs a miracle). On that fateful morning, I was a backseat passenger in a Mitsubishi Pajero, having opted to be chauffeur-driven as I needed a break from driving the regular long hours alone, traversing long distances to conduct multiple businesses. That break I took from driving almost broke my spine as I was shaken unceremoniously from my deep thoughts and felt my body snapping to attention as I jerked and jolted in the seat. Usually, I would not wear a seatbelt while in the backseat, but earlier, I had put on my seatbelt on a hunch. To this day, I don't know if this was a blessing or a curse because the neurosurgeon later told me that the damage was severe because the seatbelt strapped me in, causing me to shake like jelly. The alternative to not wearing could have been possibly death. Who knows?

As I type these words over a year later, I am in misery as I alternate between wishing it never happened and thanking God for reminding me, with pain, that at least I am still alive and walking. At the time of the accident, I was working as a real estate salesman, having taken the day off work from the pharmacy I owned and operated. I was also a registered pharmacist. The pharmacy had started to make good returns on my investment, defying all the stacked odds.

These odds included the NHF ignoring my application and a staff member at the Pharmacy Council of Jamaica stalling the final inspection because the COVID-19 pandemic had just started. I was the only person on the island who had pressed on with my desire to open a pharmacy during that period. The unsolicited diagnosis the "concerned" public gave me was that I was suffering some form of madness to embark on and persist in opening a new business during a pandemic. I was Jamaica's only new pharmacy owner when I opened on April 8, 2020. I kept the pharmacy opened and did real estate work by juggling, fasting, and praying.

Whenever I felt my faith was slipping, I asked God to preserve my soul and strengthen my faith. I asked each day for strength, patience, and endurance, to the point that my husband said that for God to give me those things, He had to give me a lot of problems and tests to mold me. I was irritated the day he pointed this out, as I believed I had endured enough tests and trials in my lifetime up to that point. I was a seasoned pit occupant, and even with my persistent spirit, I could do with a pit break. However, my husband's words held some forethought.

One of the reasons I was deemed "mad" by all except my husband and children is that when I opened the pharmacy, I was over 8 million JMD in debt and arrears because I took unpaid time to study real estate and cut my working hours. The bank had called both loans that I previously paid quite easily. I entered two multimillion dollar businesses with God behind me. I am a risk taker and a visionary, and the average person usually cannot see the method to my madness. Still, God has endowed me with multiple gifts and big visions, and sadly, these gifts attract numerous attacks that have plunged me into various pits. Like a ninja turtle, I have spent my life jumping from one pit to the next.

The bank repossessed my vehicle during the second week I opened the pharmacy. I needed this vehicle to operate my real estate business and the pharmacy, especially since only essential workers were allowed on the road. Hence public transportation was not an option. This was not good as I spent long hours at the pharmacy and worked out of the parish for some days doing real estate. At this time, I got closer and more personal with God. If I was to pull off any of my endeavors, God had to move from the backseat to the driver's seat and take me through.

I hired an accountant in July 2020, and she was dumbfounded when she first went through my books. It was mind-boggling for her to fathom how I survived since I refused to take a salary and just took money from the business for my essentials. I reinvested over ninety-five percent of the profit into the business. I told her that I managed because I understood what it meant to "Pray without ceasing." (1 Thessalonians 5:17) and have faith as small as a mustard seed (Matthew 17:20). Praying without ceasing doesn't mean that we should pray about the same problem every day, but in everything, God should be a part of our lives—every decision-making process, and goal we pursue. I told her that because of my faith, I knew that when I prayed, God answered, so I live believing that He has answered my prayer the way He sees fit, and I worry about nothing because I trust Him as the CEO of my life. Whenever I needed anything, God provided it just when I needed it most. Hence, this song has been the theme of my life:

Just when I need Him, He is my all,

Answering when upon Him I call;

Tenderly watching lest I should fall,

Just when I need Him most.

Just when I need Him most,

Just when I need Him most,

Jesus is near to comfort and cheer,

Just when I need Him most.

I recommitted my life after not being a member of any church for over eighteen years. I had vowed in all that time never to affiliate with any religious groups and never make monetary contributions, even offerings, to any church. Instead, I worked with charities for many years, helping others directly. I used to feel that the Holy Spirit wasn't dwelling in any Seventh Day Adventist Church, especially the one in my community, until I had an encounter with God one morning I decided to visit. I got baptized the following week, and the attacks intensified with my business and health.

By the summer of 2021, the pharmacy was doing very well despite all odds until one early Friday morning in July. I received a call from a staff summoning me to come quickly because on opening the building, they realized there was a break-in and robbery. In the weeks following, I lost hundreds of thousands of dollars from having to close an entire day while the police started investigations and then having to deal with the issue of raw sewage running through the business for days beginning the morning after the break-in. The money and gadgets taken were insignificant compared to the losses incurred days after the robbery. These were some of the worst times I had in business and my life as a Christian.

Interestingly, I had visited the doctor the night before the robbery as I was not feeling well. To my shock and dismay, he told me I was having an anxiety attack brought on by stress. I had been through so much that I found it amusing. Why now? I had managed to escape all my other stress episodes without an anxiety diagnosis. Guess all my pit-hopping had caught up with me. I related the conversation to my aunt that night; she thought the pharmacy was the problem. I told her the pharmacy was the least of my problems, only to receive a call about the break-in a few hours later.

Pit Hopping

I used to have an overflow of drugs, which I bought on deals. I was able to supply my pharmacy and four others from the stock. The surplus was on the floor in my office, and the sewage spill damaged them. I lost hundreds of thousands of dollars because I could not sell or return those drugs.

I was plunged into the pit of financial distress but slowly found my footing to hop out as the pharmacy was gradually incurring profits before the accident. The accident thrust me right back as it forced me to work less and slowed down my real estate work. I could not sit up or walk for long periods. This crashed my finances once more. My mobility was hampered, and I suffered excruciating pain.

One night, my husband brought me my dinner, and I sat up to eat it. I winced as I felt my lower body burn as if it was on fire. I had to hand him the plate and recline my body on the bed. I wept bitterly in pain and frustration. How could this happen to me? I am a fighter and always find a solution to my problems. This vehicular accident had come to crash my health and my entire life.

I had been given two requests from the general practitioner to do MRIs of my back's lumbar and thoracic regions from the first week in October. I had been feeling immense pain to the point where some days, when I went to work, I had to lie on the tiles in the dispensary because it was too painful to sit up. However, I thought the pain would go away. Looking at me, you could not tell that anything was wrong. I could not afford the $82,000 to do the MRI at the time as I was earning a lot less because I was now closing the pharmacy five hours earlier than usual and opening later some days.

Waiting In the Pit

A friend had offered to use her credit card to pay for the tests. The facility near me had no online payment option, and she was pregnant and couldn't travel the four hours to get to me. I pressed on thinking I had some sixty days to get it done. However, on my birthday on October 27, 2021, I slumped on my veranda in pain and tears. In desperation, I called and made an appointment to do the two MRIs (thoracic and lumbar) in Kingston the next day. I took the four hours long journey to get there so that my friend could come and swipe her credit card to have the tests done. We got back the results earlier than expected. I learned that I had multiple disc herniations, desiccated discs, bony ossification, edema, loss of lordosis, spinal cord and thecal sac impingement, and nerve impingement. This was also the last day I could submit a claim to the insurance company, or they would not accept liability. From my T2-T3 disc downwards, I only had one normal disc left.

In November 2021, I was told by the general practitioner that if my back could be fixed, the surgery would cost over $8JMD. I had no health insurance, and the person liable for the accident had no money to compensate me. I decided not to worry but to pray about it. I told the doctor and those close to me that if I had to do the surgery, God would provide the money, and if not, things would work out either way. I started researching my condition and realized that my back would be inoperable even if I migrated because thoracic disc herniations only accounted for 0.5% to 4.5% of all disc herniations. Of that small amount, only 1.8% of those below T8 were surgically repaired. Below T2, only my T4-T5 disc was normal.

Pit Hopping

The doctor made an appointment with a neurosurgeon because, by then, according to him, my situation would only get worse to the point of paralysis. When I visited the neurosurgeon, he was honest enough to tell me that he couldn't operate on me, and like the general practitioner, he said that I would only get worse, and I would be paralyzed.

The neurosurgeon restricted me from traveling outside my parish because I refused to stay in bed. He told me that I needed to lose 50 pounds before I could walk for exercise and referred me to a physiotherapist. He said a chiropractor would push me quicker into paralysis because of the extensive damage to my back. I asked him in disbelief if the accident had caused me all that damage, and he replied yes because I was in a seatbelt, and we were hit twice and shaken like jelly.

Throughout this ordeal, I still worked. My husband and I are a team; the team was essential for everything to work, so I did what I had to do. At one point, my neurosurgeon put me on a ten-day cabbage soup diet which my husband did with me. I didn't lose an ounce. I was also placed on a keto diet. I still didn't lose any of those fifty pounds.

I walked across a river one day to do a site visit, and for three weeks after that, most of my days were spent in my bed because of the excruciating pain.

One day, a batchmate and fellow pharmacy owner called me and professed that she was a Christian. She asked if I knew how to pray. She told me to tell God what I wanted, and He would do it accordingly. I told her that that was many people's mistake, so they became disillusioned and cursed God when He didn't answer their prayers. I told her that when I pray, I ask God to let His will be done, as my wish is not necessarily His will. If Jesus prayed to His Father in Luke 22:42, saying, "Father, if thou be willing, remove this cup from me: nevertheless, not my will, but thine, be done," who was I to demand anything of God? I had faith and desired to heal, but I trusted God to have His way in His time.

With physiotherapy three times weekly, I went from tilting to one side while walking in November of 2021 to walking more upright though my back hasn't improved much. My favorite Bible verse has always been Romans 8:28, "And we know that all things work together for good to them that love God, to them who are the called according to his purpose." Throughout all the pits in my life, this has always held true. God is always working things out.

These past two-plus years of being a baptized Christian has been the roughest time of my life, but I am at peace because God is the answer throughout everything. Even with an injured spine, I still jump from one pit to the next. I am fighting through debts, business challenges, my Christian walk, a family crisis, and health, but God is able. I trust in Him wholeheartedly. I do not know my future, but I trust the One who holds it. Despite our challenges:

"God is the answer
He's always there,
Don't you give up now
He'll bear you up."

Pit Hopping

As we wait in our varied pits for deliverance, healing, and peace, let us never forget that God is waiting with us and will never leave nor forsake us.

Meet Daphine Douglas

Daphine Douglas-Grant is a registered pharmacist and a licensed real estate salesman. She is a preceptor for the Pharmacy Council of Jamaica and a mentor for the HEART Trust. She has been married for over thirteen years to Chevol, with whom she has three daughters: Anusha, Naelah, and Kalea.

Daphine and her husband have worked in charity for years and have worked together mentoring youths, providing them with education, and a safe space, guiding them along their career path, and assisting them with job placement.

She loves cooking and playing dominoes. Daphine has a passion for music ministry and sometimes ministers with her children.

CHAPTER 16

Rescued from the Pit of Abuse

I went down to the bottom of mountains; the earth with her bars was about me for ever: yet hast thou brought up my life from corruption, O Lord my God. **(Jonah 2:6)**

Sometimes we experience pitfalls, landing in diverse pits because of our choices. When we go against God's original plan for our lives, we find ourselves in deep, dark holes that echo regret, disappointment, and shame when we cry out. However, God doesn't leave us in our deep pit to languish and perish. We may board there for a while, but He delivers when we come face to face with self, acknowledge our indiscretions and learn the lessons.

One such pitfall can be that of relationships. One stumble or wrong choice can have us careening headlong off a cliff costing us a lifetime of heartache and pain. It can even cost us our life and salvation. However, thanks to God, there is always a way of escape. We can wait for deliverance; He will come through at the right time.

I was 18 years old, a reasonably sheltered teenager, and was not exposed to abusive relationships. I was very active in the church and turned my attention there. At one youth retreat, Devon approached and asked me to be his date at the banquet. I accepted. He struck me as a godly man and a prayer warrior. However, something was amiss; I just couldn't put my finger on it.

We started dating a few weeks after. He proceeded to inform me that God said that I was his wife. He was forceful with his declaration, and I had not received that revelation or any other form of confirmation. I went ahead with it as I was not communicating with God as I should have. We spoke every day. He would leave a prayer voice note in my messages every morning. I was love-bombed and felt I had found "the one." But amidst that feeling, there was a level of doubt that I could not shake. Our relationship developed fast, and he did everything I desired a man to do for me.

We attended prayer and fasting sessions frequently and had regular simple interactions for a young Christian couple. Slowly, he introduced the concept of sex, claiming that our relationship was already a marriage. I was appalled and could not find any biblical or logical reasoning to support this. Simultaneously, the mask of pretense started to slip, and the angered version of his usually sunny personality shone through.

I began walking on eggshells. In every argument, I was the only one forced to apologize. Due to his extreme outward spiritual display, he could do no wrong in the eyes of most church members. Was I the problem? Over time, I withdrew and lived in his shadow. Those closest to me who discerned the looming danger warned me to remove myself from the relationship before I lost myself. By this, I was drawn into his vortex of control and didn't know how to exit.

He started to be disrespectful to my mother. Their arguments became frequent and intense. At that point, I realized I was in an abusive relationship. The expletives were constant, along with other derogatory terms. This was no man of God; this was not what God designed for me. I knew I had to get out, but how?

In a series of conversations with my mother, she urged me to leave immediately. Recounting what I knew about abusive relationships, leaving had to be executed over small secret, precise steps to mitigate extreme damages in its aftermath. I planned that the next argument, or any form of disagreement was when I would tap out.

As with most abusive situations, the abuser is always one step ahead and dangles some form of enticement or higher levels of commitment to manipulate one into staying in the relationship when they sense restlessness. I noticed he was extremely pleasant and charming for about two weeks, and I was pulled in.

We were supposed to meet on Thursday, but he messaged me to say he couldn't make it. A part of me was joyful and relieved. His reason was that he was buying some stuff for his mother. This raised suspicion as we usually meet every evening. I called him repeatedly, and he didn't answer. When he finally picked up, he said he was heading home. This was about three hours after he told me he was heading home. I had a strong impression that he had purchased an engagement ring, hence his suspicious behavior. Or could it be that he was cheating? For some reason, the ring thought was more dominant. We were approaching our one-year anniversary. Knowing him, the latter made greater sense.

On Friday, he was extremely nice when he came to meet me. There were no snappy remarks or anything. I knew he had something up his sleeve. I went to his house, where we conversed with his mother on the patio. We were laughing about something when she asked him, "You give her yet?".

Puzzled, I enquired, "What?" He started smiling, and then I exclaimed, "You bought a ring, didn't you?"

I was both shocked and upset, but I hid my emotions. He went for the ring and gave it to me. It was beautiful. He knew I liked silver. I asked him if this was a promise or an engagement ring, and he said engagement. It all made sense, the fake changed behavior, the absences, and the weird smiles from his family. I said "yes" when I should have answered "*no.*"

I felt stuck. An engagement was never on the cards, and I felt even more trapped. I felt compelled to accept the proposal even though I wanted out because I feared the inevitable response I would have gotten if I had chosen the alternative. This delayed my plans, but my God had a way out. I continued in the relationship for another month without changing my routine. My behavior had no apparent changes, but I knew I couldn't stay.

We had arguments, but none of them were significant enough for me to take my exit. However, one peaceful Sunday afternoon, all hell suddenly broke loose. I had brought mangoes for his mother, but she did not appreciate them. Her rude remarks were that they were not suitable. My mother had sent them as a peace offering to rebuild their relationship. In a defensive and possibly snarky tone, I bit back at her.

He was nearby and proceeded to defend her. In her defense, he became consumed with anger. He hurled hurtful and damaging words toward me. His words were not enough to appease his desire to wound me, so he smacked me, and I swiftly returned the blow to his face. The altercation was like that of two men fighting. However, I was weaker. I was beaten to a pulp. His mother intervened and pushed him into the boarded-door bathroom. He ripped the door to pieces with his bare hands.

However painful and tumultuous that evening was, the cover of the pit slightly moved away. A glimmer of light and freedom shone in.

When his father dropped me home that evening, I immediately told my aunt, grandmother, and mother what had transpired. I quickly blocked him on all social media platforms and gathered my clothes on my aunt's advice. Knowing how dangerous and calculated he was, the best option was to retreat to a place of safety. The decision was to stay with her as she resided in another parish. Terrified and anxious, I began my healing journey, or so I thought. Unknown calls and messages from his other relatives started to flood in, delaying the process.

Within a month, after much turmoil, the storm calmed, and I felt free. I returned the engagement ring and other items I received and walked away without looking backward. God had delivered me!

The hardest part of the aftermath of an abusive relationship is healing. There are many broken pieces to place back together. Thankfully, I did not have to do this on my own. The Master Healer, Potter, and Physician went about gathering and restoring the pieces of my soul to its original beauty, how He created it. I was not focused on how my healing process looked to anyone else. It was messy, and people were sometimes insensitive in their remarks. But God! He heals and restores.

With the help of the Holy Spirit, I knew I had to push through. There were sleepless nights, tear-stained pillows, and even Stockholm Syndrome symptoms. At one point, I blamed myself for what happened. Thankfully, my support system protected me from falling deeper into the pit of depression.

God revealed to me individuals who were praying silently on my behalf, and for that, I was grateful. Healing is still taking place as it is a process that will take a while. PTSD is no joke! Almost seven years later, God has faithfully restored my sanity and trust and lifted me out of the pit of condemnation.

During this turbulent period, one fundamental lesson was to trust Jesus in every aspect of my life. He allows the Holy Spirit to guide us in making the right decisions, but we must incline our ears to discern and obey. Often, even with persistent warning and beckoning, we still make the wrong decisions; yet He does not leave us in the cold. He continuously seeks us and guides us back under His wings, a place of safety.

Rescued from the Pit of Abuse

There are times when all will seem hopeless - But God! Larnelle Harris' song beautifully puts everything into perspective:

Abraham and Sarah never thought they'd have a son
Then descendants came as countless as the stars
Moses and God's people had nowhere left to run
Then the waters of the Red Sea stood apart
So many times, the light of hope was setting like the sun
And it seemed to the faithful it was over, it was done
But God sees some way when miracles are well beyond our view
His Love saves the day when fear would tell us there is just no use
You can look the whole world over for the meaning of it all
For the purpose that mankind has always sought
In the end, you'll discover there is no other answer
But God

Meet Deneve Sweeney

Deneve Sweeney is a child of God who seeks to stand on His promises wholeheartedly.

As a student of writing and communication, Deneve is always interested in sharing personal experiences to empower others. Also, she provides avenues for others to do the same through her involvement in various evangelistic efforts.

Deneve is an integrated marketing communication student at the University of the West Indies, Mona campus, Jamaica, and a marketing automation and web executive for a company in Jamaica.

She hopes to impart God's love through any means possible.

CHAPTER 17

The Beauty of the Morning

For his anger lasts only a brief moment, and his good favor restores one's life. One may experience sorrow during the night, but joy arrives in the morning. **(Psalm 30:5)**

Life can sometimes feel like a never-ending race, leaving you feeling discouraged, especially when the sense of being in control seems to be slipping away. A great sense of frustration can also arise from the fact that there is no perfect formula to run this race called life, yet there is a natural progression called the cycle of life, which is subsequently the road map for life's journey. For most of my life, especially my childhood years into my teens, everything seemed to be going well and on track. I enrolled in university after finishing my A-levels studies in college and progressed well in my course into the final year. However, life took an unexpected turn in my early twenties when I experienced one of the biggest derailments of my life.

I was on this roller-coaster ride, enjoying the thrill when my cart topped over. Suddenly, my body started to feel strange, and worry crept in. As a matter of urgency, I went to the pharmacy to seek advice about my health. After I consulted with the pharmacist, I was advised to buy a pregnancy test kit, which I did. However, I left the pharmacy feeling very anxious, and my mind was restless because I had more questions than answers. I decided to travel to my friend's house, and upon my arrival, I rushed to take the pregnancy test. Waiting for the results I felt like I was on the stand in a court hearing, and when I saw the lines, it felt like the judge and the jury had reached a guilty verdict. I remember gasping for air because the results were a big shock. My cart fell off roller-coaster from the highest point into a deep pit, and yes, I sustained extensive social, emotional, and spiritual injuries. How did I get here? How am I going to get through this? What am I going to tell my family?

The test results showed that I was about three to four weeks pregnant, and it was as though I missed the safety announcements, as things escalated quickly. Nothing could prepare me for the strain, discomfort and pain I would endure in the months that followed. Juggling pregnancy and my studies were very challenging. In the first trimester, I experienced morning sickness, headaches, and extreme tiredness, which meant that I could not attend lectures and complete group assignments. I fell behind on some of my modules, and the workload became increasingly challenging to manage. Subsequently, I could not complete my studies. I was forced to postpone my final year, and it was devastating not being able to finish my course as expected and graduate with my classmates.

I love to smile and stay positive; however, my circumstances and challenges stole my joy, and I was buried in a bottomless pit of despair. My usually sunny, bright, and cheerful personality took a trip and mostly left me with dark clouds of frowns and sighs. I often hid in the privacy of my room, bathroom, kitchen, or anywhere I could be alone so that no one could see the tears flooding my face. I became very good at hide and seek. I always did my best to wear a smile, so no one could tell that my heart was broken. My smile was a mask to cover the ugliness of pain, hurt, shame, regret, discouragement, fear, and unforgiveness, which I was battling deep within. Many times, I was in a battle against myself, fighting self-criticism, guilt, and shame.

As the months progressed and my pregnancy began to show, I started experiencing intrusion of my privacy. Before this, only a small close circle knew my condition, and I felt comfortable around them. Gradually, my secret was exposed, plastered on the informal headlines, and I could see judgment in the eyes of everyone who looked at me. This left me feeling extremely uneasy under the x-ray vision of their piercing eyes. Many stones were hurled, surprisingly, from folk I least expected. I felt very lost and confused in public places. It appears everyone was judging me, and I intentionally avoided people as much as possible.

I had seemingly committed the worst crime, and suddenly, my family and I were forced to deal with people's unsolicited criticisms, judgment, and unkindness. Some had taken it upon themselves to become God's unofficial spokesmen and spokeswomen. I was mercilessly condemned and shamed for my condition. This was a harrowing experience. I was heartbroken because I could not protect the people I loved during these difficult moments.

There was also a distinct shift in the atmosphere at church; some people's attitudes made me feel I was no longer welcome. Subsequently, I was no longer permitted to continue with some of my responsibilities, and my membership was revoked. This was the most painful of all the consequences.

There were so many challenges during my pregnancy I became very anxious, just considering the potential impact the added stress would have on mine and the baby's health. These stressful situations left me feeling hopeless, vulnerable, and overwhelmed. During these times, I would seek a quiet place to be alone to find peace. In silence, tears became my desperate and sincere prayers as I poured out my heart and pain onto God even though I felt unworthy. God, in His caring and loving nature, heard my unspoken prayers. I am very grateful that I could feel God's presence through the power of His Words in my brokenness. God's promise in Psalms 30:5 became my reality because whenever I was distressed, God drew closer to me, and I felt great comfort and peace from His everlasting love, grace, and forgiveness.

At times, during in my pit of brokenness and pain, I felt disconnected from God. The trials and tribulations, choices, and decisions I had made in the past, had created barriers. When all hope seemed lost, God called out to me, and as the story of the prodigal son found in Luke 15:11-24, God assured me that my past mistakes were not held against me. God embraced me with His perfect Fatherly love, and through His forgiveness, I began to feel a sense of belonging as His daughter. I trusted God's promises in John 3:16-17 and step by step, God helped me to let go of pain, hurt, unforgiveness, anger, guilt, shame, self-blame, and self-pity. I am very thankful for my healing journey thus far because I am experiencing God's amazing love and the joy of the morning in different aspects of my life.

On September 3, 2015, I alighted from my pit of shame and despair. My roller-coaster ceased, and I ended a painful era and entered a new world. In the early morning hours, around 2 am, I gave birth to my precious and handsome son. I had been in active labor for several hours, and at the very last moment, a doctor was called to carry out an emergency procedure because both of our lives were at risk. Suddenly, the room was full of professionals to assist the baby and me. As soon as my baby was born, he was quickly placed on my chest for a couple of minutes and then rushed to the children's ward for necessary check-ups and observation. I received some treatment and was left to rest because my body was exhausted.

In the early hours of the morning, I visited my son. He was placed in my arms, and I looked at his beautiful face while tears of joy flooded my eyes. I embraced my son with every fiber of my being. My heart raptured with joy, and I felt an increasing rush of love all over my body. It was one of the best moments of my life, and I will treasure the special memories in my heart forever.

Furthermore, from my experience, I can also echo the words of John 16:21, "A woman when she is in travail hath sorrow because her hour comes: but as soon as she is delivered of the child, she remembereth no more the anguish, for joy that a man is born into the world." The birth of my son is the most significant symbol of God's everlasting love for me because He never gave up on me. He qualified me to become a mother even when I felt unworthy.

John 8:3-8 tells the story of the woman who was caught in the very act of adultery. The intentions of her accusers were plain as they brought her before Jesus for judgment. Most people who read this story focus on the fact that she pleaded guilty to the sin. I can relate to this story. I wonder what circumstances led her to this unfortunate situation. We never hear her side of the story. Based on my pit experiences after falling pregnant, I sometimes wished I had a fair chance to explain myself, wondering if people would be compassionate and maybe consider the hidden factors of my untold story.

The story of the woman's background may have been known to her accusers and those wanting to condemn her, but it is evident by Jesus' response that He knew everything about her life. The people were ready and waiting to carry out the judgment they were sure Jesus would make, but they did not get the results they were hoping for. Instead, Jesus proved to be a righteous judge and met her at her point of need. When the woman stood before Jesus, it was most likely the utmost shameful moment of her life; nevertheless, at her lowest point, she received the gift of salvation by forgiving her sins. Similarly, the birth of my son was the greatest symbol of God's everlasting love for me, as He never gave up on me and blessed me to be a mother even though I felt unworthy.

Had the lady in the story not been caught, she may have continued on a destruction path, and had she not met Jesus, her ending would have been very different. Looking back on my life, I thought I had it all figured out. Before the derailment, I had planned to graduate in the summer of 2015, then transition into work to gain experience. I had also prayed that I would meet a God-fearing man and fall in love, get married, and start a family. My sudden descent into motherhood was a surprise. But in hindsight, I can testify that this sudden derailment, like the woman in the story that received salvation from Jesus on the day of her trial, was the greatest blessing of my life.

As I look back and draw parallels between the woman's story and mine, whose name remains unknown, I understand why certain situations were so difficult to deal with. At times I felt I had become invisible, no longer recognized by people I knew and loved. Like the woman in the story, my identity was wrapped up in how they now chose to see me, the different titles, labels, and false reports about me. Furthermore, I was also fighting within myself to know who I was and who I was destined to be. As a result, I learned I had to seek God more and, through his Word in Proverbs 16:2, I learned to trust His perfect will.

"All the ways of a man are clean and innocent in his own eyes [and he may see nothing wrong with his actions], But the LORD weighs and examines the motives and intents [of the heart and knows the truth]. Commit your works to the LORD [submit and trust them to Him]. (Amplified version)"

I share my story as an encouragement to someone, letting them know that there is always hope and that God is always ready, willing, and able to help us through our pit experiences. When I look at the lives of my wonderful sons—my young kings, I am in awe of how God uses my children to bring blessings into my life and many others. Each pregnancy and birth have become pillars of faith because lives are miracles and a constant reminder of God's abundant love and mercy. Secondly, I hope that through my own experiences, people will be moved to treat those with children outside of marriage with love, understanding, and compassion, in the same manner, God treats us when we sin, "For God did not send his son into the world to condemn the world but to save the world through him" John 3:16-17.

One of the ways in which God speaks to me is through songs, and my journey into motherhood and my pit experiences can be summed up by the song "Through it All" by Andrae Edward Crouch.

"I've had many tears and sorrows
I've had questions for tomorrow
There's been times I didn't know right from wrong
But in every situation
God gave me blessed consolation
That my trials come to only make me strong

Through it all
Through it all
I've learned to trust in Jesus
I've learned to trust in God

The Beauty of the Morning

Through it all
Through it all
I've learned to depend upon His Word

I've been to lots of places
I've seen a lot of faces
There have been times I felt so all alone
But in my lonely hours
Yes, those precious lonely hours
Jesus let me know that I was His own

Through it all
Through it all
I've learned to trust in Jesus
I've learned to trust in God

Through it all
Through it all
I've learned to depend upon His Word

I thank God for the mountains
And I thank Him for the valleys
I thank Him for the storms He brought me through
If I'd never had a problem
I wouldn't know if God could solve them
I'd never know what faith in God could do."

Prayer: *Thank you, God, for being the Author and Finisher of my life story and for your endless blessings upon my wonderful children. I am thankful because you have lifted us out of many pits, and I am more confident today than ever that you will lead us to run and finish the race of life with excellence. Father God, I thank you for my healing journey, and I pray for the healing* *journey of my children. Lastly, Father God, please restore and rebuild all families to withstand the testing times of this world and be victorious in all things through the mighty powerful name of Jesus. Amen*

Meet Maria Urassa

Maria is from the beautiful country of Tanzania in East Africa within the African Great Lakes Region. She now resides in the UK, a country she has grown to love and now considers a second home.

She is a devoted mother of three lovely boys, David, Josiah, and Solomon, who are a precious gift from God.

Maria dreams of using her degree in Business Management to start a charity organization to help orphaned children and families who find themselves in difficult circumstances.

She is passionate about serving God and driven to share her story, poems, and testimonies, as examples of God's everlasting love, to many people so that they will come to know and embrace their identity as sons and daughters of God.

CHAPTER 18

Will I Ever See the Light of Day?

Fear thou not; for I am with thee: be not dismayed; for I am thy God: I will strengthen thee; yea, I will help thee; yea, I will uphold thee with the right hand of my righteousness. **(Isaiah 41:10)**

One of the most horrifying pit stories I have heard is one in which a sixty-six-year-old man was robbed of cash and car at gunpoint in St. Catherine, Jamaica, and then thrown in a pit by his assailants. He was imprisoned for four nights and three days before the police and men from the fire department rescued him. This was in May of 2021. As I watched the video of the rescue, I was torn between joy and deep mental agony. Joy, because the victim survived! Agony because I could not grasp the depth of the cruelty of those who threw him in the pit. It's heart-wrenching, but the glorious reality is that he survived! Glory to God!

The victim told how he spent his time in the pit praying for deliverance. And today, he is a living testimony of the reality that 'we pray, and God delivers.' You and I can only imagine the horror of that man's real reality. He was not let down; he was thrown or dropped in that pit, which I understand is over sixty feet deep! That is one of the realities of a pit experience. It is not something you are gently placed in. It is usually an act of aggression and brutality that takes you below the surface. Usually, the intent of being pitted is that you are not just to die, but your death must be slow, physically, and mentally painful, agonizing, and wretched. Those who pit you are void of feelings for others, and pity and mercy are usually on cold storage for them. You are not expected to have a smooth fall or a soft landing when thrown into your pit. You are expected to be so battered and broken when you reach pit bottom that you should only feel pain after that to be relieved only by death.

Light is absent from the pit, and life is not expected. Darkness is present, and death is expected. Getting out of the pit is usually dependent on others. In the case of the victim, it was the police and fire department personnel. In the much-referred-to account of Joseph, it was the same folk who threw him in that took him out, not to save him, but to sell him.

An undeniable reality is whether one falls or is thrown into a pit, a pit experience is not a sweet and wonderful experience in and of itself, even if it has a glorious ending. Just think of what the likely habitats of a pit (hole) are! Just imagine what may be at the bottom of such a horrible place! And with the absence of light and the thickness of the darkness, one is just destitute! The reality is as it is with the physical or literal pit in a hollow of the earth's crust, so are circumstantial pits in life, which people either fall into or are thrown into, from which they need to be lifted. Some folks have many and varied kinds of pits in their lifetime, in which they experience all sorts of horrors and traumas, even though they seem to be okay and are living normal lives. Often an okay-looking smile on a face or the "I am good" or " I am great" talk is nothing more than a shout from deep pits for help but cannot be translated by untrained eyes or ears.

It seemed my lot to have been gifted a field with the pits of disappointment. From one to another, to the next to yet another, I have been in and out of the pits of varying depths and magnitude of disappointment. Of course, the altitude of one's expectation determines the magnitude of one's disappointment. In other words, the higher the expectation, the greater the disappointment. For Adventists, October 22, 1844, is air marked as the "Great Disappointment" because some folk listened to a preacher rather than to the Bible, who convinced them that that date was the date for the second coming of Christ. They believed and prepared, with high expectation and anticipation, but got a high magnitudinous disappointment, which shook many of their faith. *"Expectation is the mother of disappointment."* This is why the only person who will never be disappointed in life is one who has no expectations or the person who would have a hundred percent fulfillment of expectations. Zero expectation equals zero disappointment.

Upon graduation from West Indies College on May 27, 1984, with a B.Th., I was ready to join forces with those already on the ground, involved in building up the Kingdom of God, but I was shocked to find myself in the pit of disappointment, rejected on the premise that there was no room for me in the inn. This is after I sat as a youth in the church and repeatedly heard pastors, including conference personnel, pleading with parents to send their children to Adventist learning institutions to have them trained for work in the gospel ministry.

This is after I was taken out of eleventh grade from a government-run secondary school and sent back to seventh grade in an Adventist church school, upon the advice of the pastor because he saw the potential in me to become a pastor and 'Babylon' school education would not fit me for that possibility. This is after that same pastor advised my parents to send me to West Indies College High School for two years so that my mind would be thawed from the government schooling I had. Back then, every word that fell from the pastor's mouth was directly from God.

In my final year of training, I was again sitting with this same pastor before me as an instructor for two courses. I was destined to have him as an instructor, it seems. He was my instructor in the church school, Pathfinder club, college, and post-grad. But upon my graduation from college, this pastor did not know who I was, and he was not the only one who knew me that did not know me when it mattered. Someone more favored was in the mix for employment. I was thrown headlong into a pit, I tell you. My expectation was at a high altitude, and the magnitude of the disappointment was high on the scale. I lost reason, common sense, purpose, and will in that pit of disappointment. I was a shell without substance. I lived those years like a dog that lost its bone but got soaked in that process. One does not see in the dark of the pit, and in that dark pit of disappointment, I made the biggest, most regrettable, unfixable, unrepairable mistake of my life. Whenever I watched a show or movie with a time machine, I wished it were reality, to erase or undo what I did then in the dark of my pit. Even though I was finally lifted out of that pit in January 1987, the indelible effects are there.

If only the church as an organization knew how many have been flung into pits of despair and disappointment and have consequently done foolishly in a bid to get out, maybe it would act differently. I say maybe because when you sometimes think that you have gotten rid of Ahab, Manasseh is waiting.

Having been lifted from my pit, I could breathe fresh air again. I started to put the pieces together, and gradually, I was able to live with myself and others without being judgmental and fearful. I even lost more and more of an aggressive temperament, and I was gaining traction and composure.

I had established a fine family, and I was sure I was finding a purpose that would assure me that I was contributing to the good of humanity and the cause of God. In 2002, I was responsible for family ministries at the conference I served. Subsequently, I became convinced that I could make my best contribution in that area of ministry, so I started to build my hope. I would soar to a new level in this critical area of humanity. I was inventive, sometimes even unconventional, because it was clear that I wanted different and better. I had confidence in what I was about. I had a supportive queen and two princesses. And then, it all happened, without warning, not only the carpet but the floor was removed from under my feet, and I fell in and down into another horror pit.

I lost grounds for ministering to families! How could I talk to folks about what I failed in? It matters not who is to blame. It was just a colossal failure, the collapse of every wall, the shattering of every pane of glass, and a devastating crumbling of every structure erected. Would I ever see the light again, I wondered? I was lifted out but severely wounded. I smiled like I was not feeling pain, but it was a misinterpreted smile. I was hoping now to survive and move on from the pit of divorce disappointment when I was hurled into the deepest of disappointment pit yet.

There is a cause for everything that happens under the sun. However, if I tell you that I know the reason or reasons why I was set upon and targeted by the administrators of the administration for which I worked for over twenty-seven years, I would not be speaking the truth. I have not yet been told, so I still do not know the truth. In one instance, my files were contaminated with letters with false, spurious, and mischievous information because, between at least two of the administrators, there was the intent to build a case against me for my dismissal. Upon discovering that plot, I was forced to seek the intervention of

higher authorities. The intervention resulted in me getting a letter asking me to comply with the demand from the leadership of the conference to make a public apology for telling one of the administrators in the plot that they were wicked and notorious for having such information on my files and that it was in a bid to destroy my career. The chief administrator was instructed to remove the letters from my files. I hear that they were removed.

To date, I cannot confirm that because after repeated requests to the then-secretary and those who followed, I am still looking to get a copy of my files, even though it is due to me.

The first plan did not work, so plan B was activated and worked like a charm. I was presented with a letter that the executive committee voted to remove me from pastoral duties immediately, citing one reason which bore half a truth and another which was "rubbish." It did not matter to the committee that I was not given a warning or a hearing because they were all like sons of Belial, hired to carry out the dictates of the one who empowered them by giving them seats and portfolios in his cabinet. I appealed against the action taken against me, only to receive a letter from the secretary stating that the executive committee of the conference voted to rescind the decision taken prior. No reason was given for the rescinding, but most significantly, I was not returned to pastoral duties.

In one way, I am out, but in another, I am still in that God-forbidden pit, dug in the soil of hate and vindictiveness, and littered with the garbage of

falsehood, deception, and lies but kept covered by organizational corruption. Between the latter part of October 2023, and February 2014, I spent my darkest days/nights in that pit. Of all the pastors serving that conference, including departmental directors, only ONE was kind enough to stop by the pit to find out if I were still alive. Nobody else cared, or even if they had sympathy, they could not or dared not empathize with it in fear of the roaring lion who ruled the jungle then. When I appealed to the general conference president, he was too busy or occupied to deal with my insignificant complaint, so he referred me to his assistant, who told me it was not in his portfolio, so he deferred to the hierarchy of unions who differed to the very ones who determined my execution without trial. And what happened? More lies, withholding of salary,

more pressure, more torture, more provocations, more dehumanization.

I was the walking shell of a man; how have I kept my sanity to this day? Ask God. I endured hell alive as I contemplated what was happening with my children and relatives. And that is one of the reasons why I still say, in one way, I am out but still in. The mortal wound my children and my ailing father sustained at the time is permanent damage! And although I know it was the result of an evil device, I still take responsibility for their hurt. Folk on the side of the fence say, forget it, but what does forget it means? I don't have amnesia, and I hope that that will never be, so if it is true that memories don't leave as people do, then it is not likely that I will ever forget this hellish pit. I have personally written to people who were a part of the executive mob, but to date, not one single one of them responded. I was robbed of having the privilege to father my children during their troublesome teen years, and I have not seen them face to face since 2012 as a result of being pitted by my brethren! I was stripped of over two million Jamaican dollars worth of value, plus my prized preacher's Bible and hymnal, as the mob sought to establish evidence to destroy.

While I spent my time in the dense darkness of the pit, enduring its sting and infestations, folk on the outside who could assist never came to my rescue. Folk who knew the truth kept silent but reportedly lied to the chief executioner. No one I know of in the ranks of holy men came to the opening of my pit to pray for my deliverance. I was like a ghost, a leper, or contaminated with COVID. Before my experience, I could never dream that so much hate existed in: what we call church. Joseph was hated by his brothers because they were threatened by his dreams, which threatened their position as older brothers. And come to think of it, the brother that should have felt threatened more than anyone else, Ruben, by virtue of being the firstborn, was not in the plot to kill or sell Joseph! But why was I pitted? I was not threatening anybody's position. I was never running for any office at any time. Maybe like Mordecai, I was never bowing down to the Haman of the West, and that you will of necessity kill me for, either on yonder gallows or in thither pit or furnace or den, but I will willingly bow my knee to God and God alone.

With regularity, Joseph's pit experience is a popular reference point, but I believe Jeremiah's experience was more horrendous. Take some time to read the account in the 38th chapter of the book of Jeremiah, from verse one to verse thirteen. I felt like I was sinking into the mire of my pit experience, and I wish there were an 'Ebed-Melech' who would have pleaded for my life. How did I get out? You may have heard the story about the farmer's mule or donkey that fell in a pit on the farm. The pit was an old well but no longer had water. The farmer and company decided that since they could not get the animal out, they would fill the well with soil, covering up the animal they assumed was dead and preventing any other animal from falling in. So, they got to work throwing shovel after shovel full of earth into the pit. To their amazement, they saw the back of the animal emerging from the dark of the pit and discovered that what was happening was that as they threw the earth in, the animal shook its body, shaking the soil from its back, and the more dirt it shook off its back, the higher it was able to rise. The process continued until the animal was able to step out of its pit and limped away, injured but alive. Maybe it's more like that for me. Nobody lifted me out because I'm dead. And yeah, even after I managed to shake off all that dirt and limped away, I was pursued by my enemies to where I sought refuge to ensure that I would not be accepted in yonder place. Five years after I requested, I finally got a letter of recommendation from the leader of my former conference, and to this date, I have yet to get one from the secretary who has sat in that position for eight years. I repeatedly sought vindication, but not even a line, a yea, or nay has ever been given in response to my submitted requests. I have never been given access to my files, and when information is needed for possible employment, it is never supplied. And dear reader, this is the organization I served with distinction for over twenty-seven years before I was pitted. You will therefore see why all the other disappointments I had paled into insignificance when viewed through the lens of this latter. Furthermore, if you are reading with my lens, you should know why I am out but still in. What shall I say then?

"Do not turn me over to the desire of my foes, for false witnesses rise up against me, breathing out violence.

I am still confident of this: I will see the goodness of the LORD in the land of the living.

Wait for the LORD; be strong, take heart, and wait for the LORD." (Psalms 27:12-28:1 *NIV*)

Meet Robert Vassell

Robert Arton Vassel is a native of Jamaica, born and raised to devout Seventh-Day Adventist Christians in the beautiful parish of St. Elizabeth. His passion for people, his love for mission and ministry, and his desire to get deeper into the Word of God led him to pursue tertiary education at the West Indies College, earning his B. Th. He then matriculated to Andrews University, earning an MA in Religion.

He served the West Jamaica Conference of SDA for 27 years as a district pastor and departmental director: for family ministries, communication, youth ministries, prayer ministries, and ADRA coordinator.

CHAPTER 19

The Pit of Pain and Suffering

"Beloved, I wish above all things that thou mayest prosper and be in health, even as thy soul prospereth." **(3 John 1:2)**

When a seed is planted, it probably feels like it's discarded in a dark pit, buried, and left for dead (just like Joseph by his brothers), unaware of its future potential. If a seed could talk, it'll probably ask, "Why am I here?" It would possibly wonder, *will anything good come out of me?* Sometimes I felt like a lonely seed buried deep underground in pain and suffering, wondering if I'd ever be released from this prison and questioning if anything good would come of me.

I started my menses at age ten. I was in primary school in my last year, in what we call standard five in my twin island Republic. I can't remember my mother giving me a talk, but I do remember her giving me a little leaflet, "On becoming a woman," or something like that. Until age 24, the monthly visitor came regularly, sometimes heavy, but with no unusual pain. However, my life changed in the prime of my youth. I was not married yet, but I was soon to meet my future husband. I remember the day as if it was yesterday. I was at my first job post-university, and while on my menses, "out of the blue," one would say, I started doubling over in pain at my desk. My colleague had to take me home. From that day on, I started suffering from excruciating monthly pains. Other symptoms soon joined the party, such as nausea, gas, back pain, bladder pain, vomiting, and diarrhea, sometimes simultaneously. The horror!

Things had taken an awful turn, and I visited numerous doctors for several years without a diagnosis. The frustration was real. I don't know if doctors feel that patients have a bottomless pit of finances, but I firmly believe that there should be some money-back guarantee if you are unable to give me a diagnosis after I have paid my hard-earned money, but I digress.

I eventually found out what was causing my debilitating and indescribable pains. A condition called endometriosis, known as endo for short, had thrust me into a deep abyss of pain and suffering month after month, and to date, I still suffer in that pit. What is endometriosis? How did it change my life for the worse, and can it change it possibly for the better? It is a terrible condition that wreaks havoc on the body. Endometriosis occurs when tissue like the lining of the uterus is found in places outside of the uterus. The cause of endometriosis is not fully understood though several strong theories exist. However, I can sum its symptoms up in one

The Pit of Pain and Suffering

word—PAIN: debilitating, excruciating, indescribable, out-of-this-world PAIN!

I would be unwell and still have pain for several days following my period. Thankfully, those days were bearable, so I could make it through the hectic lifestyle of corporate life with no one knowing how much I used to suffer. It used to be an exhausting experience, but I never wanted it to affect my demeanor and personality as everyone knew me to be cherry and positive. I still went to work smiling, thanking God for life following those awful days. I used to pretend to use the "Men in Black" flashy thing to erase the bad memories and move on with life (I Googled and found it's called a neuralyzer).

Many times, I would ask God, "Why me?" What did I ever do in life to deserve this?" During this trial, my favorite Bible verse became Romans 12:12, "Rejoicing in hope, patient in tribulation, continuing instant in prayer." As long as there is life, there's hope, right? I woke up every day with renewed hope, asking God for the strength and patience to endure, and I have never stopped praying for healing. Endometriosis helped my prayer life if I can put it that way. It was and probably still is the biggest hurdle in our marriage, but it also helped our prayer life and strengthened us as a couple. Night after night, my husband and I would be up praying. I distinctly remember us falling asleep on our knees one night. I also learned Bible verses and claimed promises like never before. Another Bible verse that kept me and continues to keep me is Jeremiah 29:11: "For I know the thoughts that I think towards you saith the Lord, thoughts of peace, and not of evil, to give you an expected end." Yet another powerful promise was, "Beloved, I wish above all things that thou mayest prosper and be in health, even as thy soul prospereth." (3 John 1:2). So clearly, God wanted good things for me, so what was all this suffering about? There must be a bigger reason.

As time ensued, I got sicker and sicker. The pain worsened, and I started having severe chest pains. The worst part was when I started experiencing pain whenever I breathed. I started breathing shallowly because the pain was unbearable. Imagine being unable to lie down while sleeping, sometimes up to ten days per month. I had perfected the art of sleeping upright at nights on end. By this, every other aspect of life was affected, and we kept praying for a breakthrough. Keeping social appointments was not possible, and I don't believe people understood the level and intensity of my pain and suffering when I used to say, "Sorry, can't make it, my period is coming," or was here or just ended. That was like half the month!

In 2016, I couldn't take the suffering anymore and gave in to the decision for surgery, hoping that this would finally solve my problems and give me my health back. Boy, was I wrong? I had what they call in the medical world a laparotomy. The doctors cut me open and were surprised at what they saw. All my organs were fused, and seeing they were unprepared for such extensive surgery, they sewed me back up. Talk about a low, lonely moment in this pit of endometriosis. I had finally decided to do surgery, praying for all to go well, and it was a big failure. I did not know what was next for me. I curled up in that hospital bed and cried my eyes out. I felt as though God had abandoned me.

The Pit of Pain and Suffering

How did I get through the difficult moments? God reminded me of what He said in Deuteronomy that He would never leave me nor forsake me. For comfort, I sang hymns. The lyrics and melodies soothed my soul. My husband was and still is a pillar of strength and indefatigable support. I'd like to say that we had to take those marriage vows seriously very early in our marriage, "For better or worse, in sickness and in health. " We didn't know that this would be a significant test for us when we should be enjoying the honeymoon period of our marriage. Sometimes you see a couple and don't know what they're going through. When a man cleans up your vomit and wipes your poop after surgery when you cannot move your lower body, he's a keeper for sure! You must be able to rally out those tough times together when they come. It sounds like it's easy, and we were on top of things all the time, but we weren't. Sometimes we asked ourselves if God even heard our prayers, and we cried a lot together. God has kept us together; through it all. We have found our happy place, making the best of our moments together. Godliness with contentment is a great gain (1 Timothy 6:6).

The following year, in early 2017, I experienced one of the most painful moments and felt like screaming down the streets and corners of the neighborhood. No painkiller or prayer seemed adequate to ease my pain. That was the lowest point in my life, and I cried to God, "Help me, lest I die." It was just too much to bear. I had to find a way out of this misery, affecting my work, social, and mental health.

I then started researching surgery options and decided that I was going to the USA by God's grace as they were the best for multi-organ endo surgery. There was no way I was going to suffer another failed surgery, and if I was going to have it, I was going to have the best. My family asked how I would make up such a sum to pay for the surgery, and I had no idea then. I said that if God wanted me to live, He would provide. At that time, there was a severe US dollar shortage on my small island, and people were doubtful that I would get the funds I needed. I didn't know how much money I needed, but I estimated USD$40,000, which was quite a lot of money, especially when you had none. But God.

As soon as that low moment was over, I mailed my application form to the hospital in the USA via registered mail, and they said it would take three weeks. Three weeks to the date, I sent an email enquiring if they got it, and the same afternoon, they replied that it came that very day. Praise God! The day after, the doctor called me at 9 pm to say they could help me and that it would be a long and challenging multi-organ surgery. This was April 2017, and so the faith test started. The office then called with a surgery date of July 6, and I had 24 hours to reply with confirmation having no money to spare. I answered the following day with the minimum payment using Mastercard.

What a moment! I didn't know how the Lord would do this, but He said to ask, and you shall receive and come boldly. "Let us therefore come boldly unto the throne of grace that we may obtain mercy and find grace to help in time of need." Hebrews 4:16. Remember that this was April, and the surgery was in July, so we had two months to make up the US40,000. We did not know how this would happen, but we knew that God wouldn't let us down. He said knock, and the door shall be opened, seek and you shall find. (Matthew 7:7) I am still determining where I got the faith from. Heb 11:1 "Faith is the substance of things hoped for, the evidence of things not seen." There was nothing I possibly saw that confirmed that God was going to answer the prayer. I walked by faith, not by sight. I kept saying "I'm a child of the King, my Father is rich, He will provide through his people," and not once did I doubt. Once, someone asked, "What if you don't make up the money? Then what?" My reply was, "There is no 'what if'...If God wants me to live, He will provide."

We hosted two fundraisers and received donations from church, friends, family, well-wishers, and GoFundMe. The name God gave me for the fundraising campaign was #nevergiveup. Miraculously, we gathered the money by the end of June, the week before surgery. Now the fact that this took place was a miracle. First, that figure was a guesstimate. It turned out to be almost the amount we needed. When things get tough, I reflect on that campaign and that God told me to "never give up."

One of the other key lessons I learned through this trial is total reliance on God, even though sometimes I may falter and doubt. Every single time, God reminds me. "But seek first the kingdom of God and his righteousness, and all these things will be added to you." (Matthew ESV) I mean, who am I going to serve after all this? I told God I would serve Him for the rest of my days if He saved my life. God provided and continues to provide for our every need, and He meant it when he said He would supply all our needs (Philippians 4:19).

Before I left the country, I was walking like The Hunchback of Notre Dame, not entirely understanding the source of my hunch.

Waiting In the Pit

When I got to the USA, I had to visit the thoracic surgeon, who told me that my lung was 2/3 filled with fluid and functioning at 20% and that he may have to do two surgeries. I then learned and understood that the pressure on the lungs caused the pain, making me hunch over. I calmly told the surgeon without flinching, "Do not worry; God is with us." The surgeon looked at me as though I was crazy.

The surgery lasted eight hours, an entire workday, and I only had one done. They separated all the organs millimeter by millimeter through keyhole surgery and with the aid of robots. They drained 2.3litres of fluid from my right lung. I also lost the lining of my right lung and 2cm of my diaphragm. They said that I had come just in time. That was God's miraculous timing. Hallelujah!

The nurses were terrific. They were very encouraging through it all, and that's how we should approach life. Following surgery, I had to do breathing exercises to expand my right lung again, as no one knew how long the fluid compressed it. I would blow the spirometer, and it would hardly move. The nurse exclaimed, "Good job!"

I knew I wasn't doing well, but I appreciated the positive cheering. Post-surgery, I didn't want to get out of bed to walk and had a mini meltdown. The nurse sat patiently and counseled me. When I used the walker, they would say, "Wow, you look so great; look at you powering down that hallway!" I knew it was all part of their training, but I felt the compassionate love of Jesus through their kindness. Shouldn't we be like this with others? Calm, patient, loving, and empathetic?

The Pit of Pain and Suffering

Every day I thank God for this new lease on life. I am eternally grateful for the sacrifices made by my aunt and mother, who were with me in the USA for two months.

Sickness and recovery give you an entirely new perspective on life. It shows you what's important. Once you have life, health, and strength, your #1 priority should be God. My heart was so grateful that I asked God, "What can I do to give back?" The response was, "Help others." This was how the FAITH Foundation for Women's Health was born. Why FAITH? Because it was birthed out of a real-life Faith experience, and the acronym stands for **F**emales **A**cting to **I**mprove **T**heir **H**ealth. Other women are suffering just as I was and praying for a breakthrough miracle in their health. Over the years, the foundation has held seminars and support group meetings for women.

Germination occurs when all the proper variables are in place (oxygen, temperature, light, or darkness), and the seed coat absorbs water, causing it to swell and rupture one day. It shoots up above the ground getting sunlight and will reach its full potential to become a flower or fruit-bearing tree. After being buried for so long, this was the fruit of my pain and suffering—Faith Foundation. My pit was a fruit pit. In my dark moments, God was preparing me to bear fruit as He held and nurtured me in the pit of His hand. My pain and suffering were the channels God used to prepare me to give back.

So, after such miracles, I would hope to be fully healed for the rest of my life, but six years post-surgery, here I am again, experiencing familiar pains. Why am I still in this pit? God is undoubtedly trying to get my attention. I feel as though He's saying, "You depend on

Waiting In the Pit

man (doctors) and medication, but you need to trust in Me. I can make you whole." Like the woman with the issue of blood, who waited for 12 years, I have been waiting for 15 years. How much longer? I cry. The tears are still real. How much longer, Lord? "I know things could be worse," I say to Him, "but please, Lord, make it better." How much longer do I have to stay in this pit? I don't want to talk about it much. I don't want people to pity me or say that I don't have enough faith and don't believe God can heal me.

Do I have faith? Of course, I do. That's how I'm alive today. A friend gave me the nickname "Faith Girl." In fact, I see miracles all the time. God paid our car insurance the same year I had major surgery in 2017. I saw a deposit on my credit card, the same amount we needed to pay the car insurance, but no one had my credit card number; surely this must be an error, so I went to the bank to make a report. The CSR checked and told me the deposit was made in my name. I was in awe. That had to be an angel. Miracles? Yes. I've seen them. Have you ever been paid in error? The organization said, "Keep the money, don't worry about it. An angel was working in the background."

In a former job, I prayed that they would send me to Paris for the training in time for my friend's wedding, and the timing was perfect! Another time I was on a plane to Puerto Rico on the first day of a new job, knowing that I had declared that previously that the next country I wanted to visit was Puerto Rico. I even had the simple request for a Julie mango fulfilled when I got home. God has answered all these prayers. I can go on and on about all the miracles and blessings I've known and experienced well. I can

The Pit of Pain and Suffering

write a book on the number of testimonies and miracles I've seen. Prayers and dreams do come true.

I know how to be abased, and I know how to abound. Everywhere and in all things, I have learned to be full and hungry, both to abound and to suffer need. I can do all things through Christ who strengthens me. So then, why am I here in the pit of endometriosis pain singing?

"Yet Still I Rise" by Yolanda Adams is the anthem of my life. I'm praying for strength to endure until God is ready to heal me. Maybe He still has me in this pit for a reason, and I still need to accomplish it. But I started the Foundation, right? Well, maybe He wants me to do more, to dig deeper. Sometimes I say I don't know what to say to God anymore. He knows my heart's desires. I'm tired of suffering but I have learned that when God is all you have, He is all you need. God wants me to seek and trust Him 100%.

I must stay positive; I can't afford to give up now. God keeps showing me that He's there with me. I've been doing more research and getting more support. *I want to be better first,* I told myself, *before I can truly help others.* But God has other plans. So, while I'm still in the pit, I know I must help others more. Through it all, He keeps me, so I will not give up.

My encouragement for you is that you should be steadfast in your pit. Never give up as you wait on God to deliver you. Learn the lessons and see how God desires to use you. You may be the inspiration another person needs while you grow in your pit.

Meet Joleen Meharris-Simpson

Joleen Meharris-Simpson was born on the twin island Republic of Trinidad and Tobago. She is a multi-lingual, qualified interpreter, and foreign language educator. She loves traveling and meeting new people.

Her favorite Bible verse is Romans 12:12, "Rejoicing in hope; patient in tribulation; Rejoicing in hope; patient in tribulation; continuing instant in prayer."

She founded the FAITH Foundation, a women's health organization, from her real-life faith experience. She hopes this chapter will help women seek early detection for health challenges while keeping their faith and trusting God. She loves traveling and meeting new people.

CHAPTER 20

Why live when you want to die?

"If a man dies, shall he live again? All the days of my appointed time will I wait, till my change come." **Job 14:14**

Where do I start? It's a miracle of miracles that I'm alive today to tell this story. I've been down the dark tunnel of overdosing on pills, drinking dangerous substances, and even attempting to jump from a building. Yep. That was me! Imagine God wanted me to live so badly that He granted me favor to stay three weeks, all expenses paid at a nearby private hospital. It was God's way of saying, "Rest, my daughter; I am not ready for you to leave this earth right now."

Depression and suicide were always two sinister friends I could not get out of my space. They have been with me since primary school, only they had more color in those days and were not readily identifiable. As the years went by, they matured and got darker and gloomy in their sense of fashion. They were so influential I started dressing and even smelled like them. Did I say smell? When you are depressed, bathing feels too close to baptism, refreshing, and renewal. Remember, I wanted to die and not live, so I welcomed the stench of rot.

It was hard for me to smile and accept the happy moments. I was drowning slowly in the quicksand of my mind. No prayers seemed to be powerful enough to save me from me. I knew God was somewhere, but I could not see Him through the haze of my negative thoughts.

I remembered faintly that my bedroom walls were all white with primer paint because my mother couldn't afford colored paint then. It was not a priority. When the glorious white sunlight peeked through my window in the morning, everywhere lit up like a treasured room in heaven. However, in my skewed mind, it felt like a 5-star hotel in hell.

I did not like life, and life did not seem to like me back. By the time I got to university, I wanted out. I embraced my doom by raising the alarm among my roommates and family by trying to commit suicide on the top floor of my dorm. God is helping me remember the details because He wants someone reading this to be healed. Depression does something to the brain where it digs a deep hole and buries all data to protect itself from the poison of the past—like hard ground, breaking to give way to a growing seed. I feel my thoughts giving way to reveal this story. I hope it bears fruit and blesses and inspires someone.

Writing now, I recall taking up my phone and telling my mother with tears choking my voice, "Mummy, if you don't come here and save me, I am going to jump, and you will never see me again." Torrents of tears wash my cheeks as I write because I have put my mother through torture and trauma too many times throughout my short life. No mother should have to embrace the pain of a depressed daughter. That morning, my cousin and her husband rushed up the highway just in time to kick down my door, ripping it off its hinges and grabbing me from the window before I fell off my hinges. They know all the details; I'm just banking on the fiber I found on the walls of my mind.

It was a hard time for my family. They couldn't trust me, and I was under constant surveillance and supervision. I was in prison. I was trapped in the prison of my mind and confined behind the bars of my emotions. What triggered it? Could it be the untimely death of my father? I had no clue. I am not a doctor, nor am I a psychologist. This chapter is simply my testimony of how I climbed out of the pit of depression and swung and landed safely from the tree of suicide. I have no clue how to relay this experience aptly. Thank God for a great editor; she does a fantastic job putting the puzzle pieces together by the grace of God. The best and most effective way to share my experience is to break it up for you.

Someone once said the questions are sometimes more valuable than the answers we give. Questions help us dig deep and go beyond the surface. I have dared myself to answer some questions so you can get a better, bigger picture of my life and my story of overcoming.

Waiting In the Pit

So, let's section off this chapter like my aunty would do when detangling my thick scrub of freshly washed 4C jet-black hair. She would part my hair into four large sections and comb out each section with moisturizer and water. That is precisely what I want to do here. I'll answer four major questions hoping that someone can be healed and get the help they need.

The questions? Let's begin with what depression was like for me. What were some of the effects of the season of depression? Then I want to layer things by providing you with techniques and strategies which helped me. Finally, I want to answer the question: is there a way to cope, and is there any hope?

What comes to mind when I consider depression is a "deep press." Depression is the high-intensity pressure we put on ourselves. It's a dark place, gloomy and lonely, with echoes of harsh words, cold steers, and people mainly verbalizing what you feel about yourself, yet, they don't seem to understand or even care. Depression for me was like self-hate on cocaine. I disliked how I looked, felt, and even how I showed up in the world. My mother was the only person who had compassion and understanding of the matter. Johanna is superhuman to be gifted with a complex daughter like me. Like the woman with the issue of blood from the Bible, she tried everything and spent her last at doctors and physicians to save me. My mother had a prayer cloth she used to kneel on to cry out to God for my health and salvation. Her knees might still have bruise marks from interceding on my behalf. Every action I performed worried my mother more and more about my life. For a season, I spent hours writing Bible verses on the walls of my room with a pencil. Then I would bite my nails till the flesh bled. I hated combing my hair, and taking a shower felt like a chore. My memory was fading, and I was silent most of the time. Fear crippled me, and I hid from anyone who came to visit and pretended most times to be asleep.

This chapter of my life saw me descending a slippery slope of destruction. Eventually, I was summoned to see the campus psychologist. She looked at me as if I was an empty shell. I would stare at her and made up responses to escape the therapy. I didn't want to be there. I was flushed with embarrassment each session. Whenever I exited the room, someone I knew would witness me walking out of the "mental healing room." Everyone identified it as the mental health room. I'd look away and act as if I was ok. Sometimes we carry our pain quoted in Bible promises, masked with smiles and "I am ok." Search the averting eyes; they usually tell a better tale.

In this season, the symptoms were mild at times and, at other times, extreme. There was a deep desire to give away money and get rid of my stuff. Other times the hoarding hormone was high, and I hid things in my room to make me feel whole and accomplished. There was a lot of emotional eating, oversleeping, and overthinking. Then came cutting off all my hair and donning various bright colors to feel present in the world. Once, I wanted to pierce the entire spine with silver rings. Someone offered to do it for free, so I jumped at the opportunity. I called my mother, asking for permission, and tried to trick her into believing it would help me feel better about myself. She responded with a deafening NO. My mother always told me yes. I didn't see this coming. It felt like a plane crashing through the world trade center of my lungs and stopping me mid-breath.

I had to devise some excuse to complete the mission of becoming the daredevil I wanted to show up as. Coming face to face with suicidal thoughts and depression makes you adopt this reckless lifestyle. You no longer value your thoughts, your feelings, or your body. Your value is worse than a rag doll. When the earrings and industrial piercing were declined, the next best idea was tattooing. I knew I wanted a reminder on my arm with the words, "Love covers a multitude of sins," to remind God that should I be successful, His love for me should cover this sin. The tattoo was supposed to be done on my left arm in case it affected my writing ability. I dreamed of it day and night—a spiral fancy thin writing which would have everyone asking to read my arm. I didn't think about the fact that I didn't have the money for a tattoo, and I was not prepared to get it poorly done by a random hole-in-the-wall canvas tattoo artist.

Remember I mentioned in this state you have no value for your body? Well, I wanted to be loved and cared for. Most people use sex and sexual perversion to escape the tormenting cage of depression. Did I have free liberal sex? No, but I wanted to damage myself so severely. I did the next hurtful thing. I led men to love me and then disappointed them with a lie that I was on my period. I am an actress and was a temptress, so they believed every lying word that dripped like honey from my lips. I never wanted a bad name, so sex was out of the picture. Flirting and kissing seemed safe, but they always left me emotionally attached to someone who didn't love me.

Did I mention I was great at showing up with several different personalities? I lived on Web MD and self-diagnosed myself with a list of mental and emotional disorders—the appetite pendulum rapidly swings from overeating to starvation. My sexual appetite was fueled by getting relief from pain through masturbation and scrolling on pornographic sites. All these became bitter to the stomach because it was all fake, and my pain was real. I GAVE UP when I realized that all these toxic strategies did not treat my situation. Life became pointless.

Thankfully, God always sends someone to the rescue. I remember it like it was yesterday. My eldest brother Gerard looked me in the eyes and said, "You need to stop performing; you need professional help." I was disappointed. He cracked my code. I was pretending and performing, and it felt safe. Yes, I was the great pretender, and my power was found in staying undetected. However, while all the acts were rehearsed, my mental health issues were as real as day.

The question remains, Candice, if these things didn't work, then what did? My brother's honesty and paying for professional help was the genesis of my healing. It was also the exodus from a system I created by ignoring God's love and doing life on my terms. The words that came from the mouth of the Christian counselor were like verses from Proverbs and songs from the book of Psalms. Slowly but surely, I began to change and crawl from my pit. It wasn't just one thing. A plethora of efforts placed me on the path toward healing.

I remember a pastor had me in his office every day. My mom dropped me off early in the morning and returned to get me after work. It was like daycare and Sunday school all in one for five days a week. When he first started counseling me, I was dead like a doornail. Nothing entered and nothing exited. However, this experience proved the power of God's Word. Even though he knew he wasn't getting through to me initially, he repeated the Word of God daily. The Holy Scriptures repeatedly read were the positive brain washing I needed. The Word of God eventually showered my mind in torrents like rain after Noah had built the ark. The flood waters of the Word tore down idols and washed away false teachings and the damaging and corrosive ideologies that held me captive. I was cleansed daily. My mentor and counselor got me to serve despite not being in the healthiest space. God used the pastor and the counselor to usher me into wholeness.

I needed to socialize, and I needed my spirituality back. The worst thing a depressed person can do is stay away from the church and isolate themselves from people. It is not healthy. Serving others got me to stop thinking about myself, and attending church helped me to rebuild my relationship with God.

"I was lost, but now I'm found; I was blind, but now I see." Depression closes your eyes to the truth and deafens you to the voice of God. I can safely say I overcame the pit of depression and suicide after God sent these professionals to pull me from my pit. I need to note that a simple change in diet, exercise, and sleep hygiene also did my body well, and I was getting to a better self that depended on the Savior.

The final and million-dollar question: Is there any hope? The answer is a resounding yes! There is hope beyond the pit of depression. I'll use the acronym HOPE to explain how you can access the rope of hope to pull you out.

H: ask for **HELP**. At first, you may not see your need for help, but if someone offers, please consider it. Ultimately only God can pull you out, but He has His agents to support the process.

O: **OPEN** your mind to treatment and professional intervention and be optimistic. 90% of the illness is in the mind. The other 10% depends on how you deal with it. A positive mind has positive effects on the entire body.

P: **PRAY** and praise God through it all. The pain is part of the process, but it was not meant to remain parked on your path. One songwriter said, "Pray your way out..."

E: **ENCOURAGE** yourself in the Lord and encourage others by sharing your testimony. You can thank God even while you are in the middle of overcoming. It's called, according to my mom, "Thanking God in advance."

I can say so much more about this experience, but it will take an entire book to tell it all. I encourage you to educate yourself about depression. Many of us think depression looks and sounds a particular way, but only when we know the signs and symptoms can we be better prepared. It can creep up at any time of your life, even when you are in your winning season. Sometimes the traumas of our past are triggers. The trauma loads the gun, but the negative approach to the thought of the trauma pulls the trigger. In that season, I can't stress enough the role self-care and coping strategies played in my victory story. Self-care made me fall in love with myself all over again. Instead of pressuring myself, I was now protecting myself and my space.

Depression and suicide are like twins joined at the chest. I want to share the four D's of dealing with this deadly twin.

1. ***Decide:*** that you want to exit this Pit. Everything begins and ends with a decision. Decide that you would not introduce any extreme practice to worsen your experience. While depressed, based on the stage you are at, it's challenging to decide. Reach out to someone you trust and bear your heart to them so that they can help you act. Decide in your mind, with whatever strength you have left, that you will decide day by day to live. Choose life and not death.

2. ***Distract:*** not all distractions are negative. Distractions can be healthy to redirect your mind in another direction. When we engage in activities that keep us distracted from our present situation, it allows our minds to think about new things. Depression can weigh us down and make us mentally drained. We may need to slow down and become more aware of the thoughts we allow to float and run wild in our minds. It's about replacing a negative thought with a positive. If we deposit negative thoughts, we can only withdraw negative words and actions. Where the mind goes, the man follows. Change your mind, and you will change the man.

3. ***Discuss:*** most of the issues we allow ourselves to live through without addressing them grows like cancer. Many

are ill because of unspoken words or emotions left unattended. We must speak with someone even if we must pay them to listen to our issues. We need people to lean on when life gets heavy—people to share our hearts with. Discussing matters with God through his Word also brings clarity. Confusion is the smoke before the fire of depression is set ablaze.

4. **Develop:** a healthy lifestyle. Applying the N.E.W.S.T.A.R.T. strategy benefits us in the long term. When we abuse our minds and bodies, illness strikes. We must incorporate healthy nutrition, daily exercise, water, sun exposure, temperance, fresh air, and proper rest into our lifestyle. When the laws of health are violated, the man is vulnerable. If you don't live a healthy lifestyle, today is a good day to start.

I am not a doctor. By God's grace, I have shared in this chapter my struggles with depression and suicide. Doctors told me that I was depressed, but I had no clue that was my state. I thought I had just been dealt a lousy hand of cards. Only a professional is fit to diagnose depression. Please don't read this chapter and think you are depressed because you resonate with it. Prayerfully seek professional help.

When overcoming depression, you need a strategy and a solid game plan. It's an enemy, and it must be defeated. We need not lean on our understanding but allow the Holy Spirit to minister to and see us through. He did it for me; He can do it for you.

Meet Candice Andrews

Candice Andrews is a woman after God's own heart. She has a practitioner's certificate in drama education and graduated with first class honors in B.A. Theatre Arts. She is known as "The Host with the Most." She serves the Most High God and gives the most value.

For the past ten years, she has been integrating her skills in performing arts to raise individual and community awareness about ways to promote a healthier awareness of self and service to God-given talent.

Candice Andrews is known as a creative, an educator, online event host and an advocate for the holistic development of girls and women. Ms. Andrews is a theatre arts teacher and recent author of the book The Stretched-out Life. She has been in the field of performing arts and workshop facilitation for over the last ten years. Her motto is one plants another one waters, and we all feel the impact.

On Instagram she goes by the name @speakwithcandice and on Facebook she is known as Candice purity Andrews.

CHAPTER 21

Waiting Well

I wait for the Lord, my soul doth wait, and in his word do I hope. **(Psalm 130:5)**

Waiting is a challenging feat. We will always be in a waiting queue as we go through life. No matter how advanced technology develops, how proficient customer service becomes, how swift AI technology generates information, or how adept mankind gets at manipulating systems and processes, waiting is inevitable. Therefore, we should resolve in our minds how we will wait. As Christians, we must learn to wait well. The word wait may seem passive at face value, but this little word is both passive and active. How do we wait while life is treading along? Do we sit still and do nothing?

While waiting, our minds and hearts must align, and we must discern the voice of God telling us when, how, and where to move. We must face each challenge and adversity daily with an attitude trained by heaven. We still have decisions to make here and now, so what do we do? We can occupy until our waiting season is over, prepare ourselves as our hearts and minds anticipate God's release, or rush through and proceed headlong in inevitable danger, destruction, and disappointment.

Sometimes God is waiting for us to move as with the children of Israel by the Red Sea. In Exodus 14, the Lord asked Moses, "Why are you crying out to me? Tell the Israelites to move on." While they were told to stand still and see the salvation of the Lord, it did not mean waiting passively and purposelessly. They had to do their part and move forward, and in their moving, God divided the Sea so they could move forward on dry land. Could this then be a faith issue or a matter of trust? Why do we have God waiting on us when He has told us to move?

When God says to wait, whining, complaining, doubting, and fearing do not make Him change His mind; in fact, they may delay the process. He knows the reason He told us to wait. Worrying and stressing only make the waiting seem longer and more agonizing than it is. Isaiah 40:31 declares, "But they that wait upon the Lord shall renew their strength; they shall mount up on wings as eagles; they shall run, and not be weary; and they shall walk, and not faint." So, teach us, Lord, how to wait and to wait well.

It took me thirteen to fourteen long years to resolve, that I needed to learn how to wait well. As I went through my crucible, it seemed like there was no end in sight. I complained and whined day after day and night after night, yet nothing changed. I still had to wait. God asks, "Who, by worrying, can add a single hour to our life?" (Luke 12:25) This shows how pointless it is to worry when worry changes nothing.

As I reflect, even though it seems as if nothing was happening during those years of waiting, marvelous things were happening below the surface. Like the Chinese bamboo, there was no action above the surface, yet the Chief Designer was intricately weaving testimonies and detailed patterns of lessons and what I call "gems of truth" that I would need to strengthen and bolster my faith in Him. I could not see it, but God was doing work within me. He was refining, renewing, renovating, and restoring me through a painstaking process of character development, refinement, and renewal, teaching me how to wait purposefully and prayerfully. God brought me out of an "89-day" jail pit that I detailed in *Waiting in the Pit Volume 1*, and I am still rejoicing and praising Him. I stand in awe daily of how faithful He's been to me.

As I have mentioned before, on life's journey, we are in constant waiting. While I write this chapter, I am currently waiting in a new pit for a few things, but the waiting process is different this time. I am waiting much better, trusting God, and not leaning to my understanding. While waiting, I seek God's guidance and process things through an "alignment testing" system according to His Word. My relationship with God has given me the confidence that, at the right time, He will grant me the desires of my heart. I stand still in my heart and mind but actively obeying God, taking care of His business, and trusting Him to care for mine. Our covenant relationship is getting stronger and stronger, giving me peace that surpasses all understanding.

This season, I am waiting in my pit of singleness for the kingdom purpose spouse and marriage God has for me. His Word announced from the beginning that it was not good for man to be alone, so God made a help meet for Adam. He created me to be the help meet for one of His precious sons, and I wait patiently (though it's not always easy). This pit of singleness gets lonely though I am not alone. It gets dark and dreary, and many times, I am consumed with the feeling that no one understands, and the questions of "Why me?" and "How long?" plague my consciousness. Being in a pit is one thing, but not knowing when or how you will get out is another creature. Sometimes you are left doubting you will ever get your heart's desire; you feel lost and get sucked into other pits such as self-pity and condemnation.

While I am waiting, I am praising and trusting God. I take care of His business by spending more time in His Word so that I can see and hear Him clearly when He speaks. He says His sheep hear His voice, and they follow Him. The only way to know His voice is to spend time with Him to recognize His voice and not follow that of a hireling or usurper. I am determined to live intentionally and purposefully, basking in God's presence and His faithful promises to me, knowing I can rely on and trust Him.

I have failed many times, but this time I am resolute to put my mind under the subjection of the Holy Spirit and surrender so that He may order my steps and keep me in alignment with His will. My focus has shifted from what I want to what pleases the heart of my loving Father. In the past, I thought I knew what was good for me, and I grossly misunderstood the concept and principle of relying on God for everything. I was drawn away by lust and enticement and didn't realize I needed to ask God about a spouse. I thought I could select who I wanted and change them if they weren't in Christ, and then we would live happily ever after; how naïve! The Word admonishes me not to be unequally yoked (2 Corinthians 6:14) for a reason, but I never read it myself nor asked for an understanding of it.

As God led me through a season of self-reflection and character refinement, the Holy Spirit impressed me to reframe and retrain my mind, and I started viewing this season of singleness through new lenses. Instead of perceiving things the way my experiences cultured and trained me to do, I am keen to hear and see what He is trying to show me. My waiting is now ordered within the parameters of how can I be the best person I can be in this world? I am living READY cultivating the fruit of the Spirit not to attract a man but to be more like Jesus. I desperately need this to be the norm of my life rather than the alternative. I desire to be a well-rounded and balanced individual allowing the Holy Spirit to lead. I figured that if I was going to be my best, I must embody the fruit of the Spirit in all areas of my life: as a mom, a child of God, an aunt, a niece, a daughter, a co-worker, a fellow motorist on the road and even as a grocery shopper. I must have love, joy, peace, patience, kindness, goodness, faithfulness, gentleness, and self-control.

I am still single now, which shows that whatever I was doing on my own was not working at all. I was leaning toward my stubborn understanding and not acknowledging God. The ungodly relationships I endured only brought me pain and misery. I was left deeply wounded, trying to pick up the broken pieces of my shattered life. I realized that a mind not under the control of the Holy Spirit only kills and steals one's joy, peace, purpose, dreams, and self-worth. In Jamaica, a saying is, "Why buy the cow when you can get the milk for free?" This addresses the idea or questions why a man would seek or commit to marrying when he is enjoying the benefits of marriage as a single person. I was performing marriage responsibilities to men who had not done the honorable thing to commit, much less ask my hand in marriage. I catered to their sexual and personal needs, cooked special meals, and even had babies.

I was left with tears, unmet dreams, broken promises, regrets, and children to raise alone. These were the harsh and brutal realities I had to face. But it was my own choices that led me to my reality, and I had to own up to it. I had wandered off like that one sheep that went astray. I had strayed, hoping to find my own pasture, not trusting that the Good Shepherd created the meadowland and would only lead me to the very best pasture. I doubted the ability of my Shepherd to take loving care of me. So, I went off believing I could find greener pasture, chasing what seemed right, forgetting that there is a way that seems right unto a man, but the end thereof is the way of death (Proverbs 14:12).

There were moments as I reflected when God left the 99 other sheep to find me and bring me back, but foolishly, I wandered off again, grazing in unfamiliar and dangerous meadows. Like the prodigal son, God's daughter forgot her royal bloodline and subjected herself to verbal and emotional abuse and substandard treatment. I fooled myself into thinking that I could somehow be good enough to influence change in another person all in my strength, failing to realize once again that my righteousness is as filthy rags and that outside of Christ, I can do nothing.

In my memoir, *Woman Straightened Up*, I detailed the weights I carried on my back that left me bent over and deformed from spiritual scoliosis. The shame and degradation that accompanied my bad choices are no longer the weight under which I am bent. I have been seen, called, and touched by Jesus and now straightened up. I am waiting in this place, and though it is sometimes uncomfortable, and I get restless occasionally, I reflect on the waiting journey. I see how Jesus has brought me through every treacherous path. He has carried this wounded sheep gently and lovingly back to the fold several times. He has never given up on me. Hence, I am empowered and strengthened to carry on. I am assured that this, too, shall pass. I will not live in my singleness forever. I am single but not forsaken. The Holy Spirit guides my thoughts and wandering mind when I muse about how miserable and lonely I am. As I stand on the edge of mental torture, He pulls me in with His staff, and I quickly change my thoughts to the truth and promises written in the Word that I have hidden in my heart.

He says He has good plans for my life to give me hope and a future (Jeremiah 29:11). He says I am fearfully and wonderfully made (Psalm 139:14) and that I should cast all my cares upon Him because He cares for me (1 Peter 5:7). I know that God is not a man that He should lie. His Words will not return unto Him void but will accomplish what He sent forth for it to accomplish (Isaiah 55:11). God has started a good thing in me, and He will bring it to completion. As I wait patiently on Him, He inclines His ears and hears my cry.

To sum this up, there are seven steps we can actively take to wait well on the Lord.

1. We need to **surrender**. We are to trust in God with all our hearts. In all our ways, we are to acknowledge Him, including believing and trusting that His ways are not our ways nor His thoughts our thoughts. When we acknowledge Him in all our ways, He assures us that He will direct our path. (Proverbs 3:5-6). Submit your thoughts, your mind, and your plans under the authority and leadership of the Holy Spirit. As Paul says, we must die daily so the Holy Spirit can move and have His perfect way in our lives.

2. Because He promises to direct our path, we ought to seek His guidance by **spending time in prayer, praise, and studying His Word**. God tells us that if we lack wisdom, we should ask Him, and He will freely give it to us. We will need wisdom and discernment during the waiting period so that we are not bombarded and pressed under the pressure of the wait, but we will have clarity of mind to make the right decisions along the way.

3. We should practice **patience**. Patience is a critical virtue in the Christian sojourn. Virtue means showing high moral standards. We will need to cultivate this in every part of the waiting process. Whether we are at the bottom of the pit, climbing out the pit, or if we have been delivered from the pit, patience will be needed. We must be patient with God, ourselves, and others, trusting and believing that while we cannot see anything above the surface, God is still working behind the scenes for our benefit. Remember, Jesus is long-suffering, which goes

farther and deeper than patience. He suffers long with us, and if He does that, we can know we are of great value to Him.

When a seed is planted, we don't see immediate growth above the soil's surface, but it grows as it is watered and nurtured. Eventually, we get to behold the results of our patience: "From a tiny seed grows a mighty oak" (unknown).

4. Your **faith needs to be developing and becoming stronger in Christ.** This waiting period can be used to deepen your faith in God as He takes us higher in Him. Trust and know that God is faithful; it's who He is. He said in 2 Timothy 2:13, "If we are faithless, He remains faithful because He cannot deny Himself." Because faith is a part of God's essence, He is dependable, never wavering, and does not falter. He will fulfill His promises concerning you and me. We are all born with a measure of faith, and Matthew 17:20 tells us that if we have faith as small as a mustard seed, we can say to the mountain move from here to there, and it will do so. If such small faith can move great mountains, imagine what increased and more immense faith can do. Do not allow the pit of heartache, alienation, suicidal tendencies, and disappointment to break your faith. Allow these burdens to build your faith instead, even though you have not seen it yet.

5. Keep and maintain your hope in Jesus. Romans 5:5 says, "And hope does not put us to shame, because God's love

has been poured out into our hearts through the Holy Spirit, who has been given to us." (NIV) In this season of waiting in the pits of sorrow, depression, shame, expectation, pain, alienation, or whatever you have been going through, remember that you still have life, which means there is hope. Lamentations 3:25 tells us that the Lord is good to those who hope in Him, to the one who seeks Him. God assures us that hope will not disappoint us because He has promised to complete the good work, He has started in us. We know this because God pours His love into our hearts through the Holy Spirit.

God's promises concerning hope can be trusted and relied on to help us wait with great anticipation and expectations, knowing that God cannot lie and that the gift of hope will turn your impatience into joy and confidence in Him. Hope in God brings Scriptures such as Ephesians 3:20 to life, "Now to him who is able to do immeasurably more than all we ask or imagine, according to his power that is at work within us." (NIV) We can conclude that God can do much more than we ever hoped. Think about the most significant thing you are hoping for, and now imagine God can do infinity times that.

6. **Trust God's timing.** As our Creator, God knows the plans He has for us, not to harm us but to give us hope and a future (Jeremiah 29:11), and because He made us, who better to tell us when to move? God is not constrained by time; He sits outside of time. 2 Peter 3:8

says, "But do not forget this one thing, dear friends: With the Lord, a day is like a thousand years, and a thousand years are like a day. 9 The Lord is not slow in keeping his promise, as some understand slowness. Instead, he is patient with you, not wanting anyone to perish, but everyone to come to repentance." (NIV) This Scripture implies that we have not even lived one whole day as far as God is concerned. I know this crucible seems like an eternity, and it keeps going, seemingly with no end in sight, but we must remember that our Great God and Father is and will always be in control.

7. Finally, **come outside of yourself and your problems and shift your mind** to focus on serving others. Remember, Jesus came not to be served but to serve. When our entire person is consumed with all the pits we are in, the enemy slithers in and makes them seem so much bigger and more insurmountable than they are. While you passively wait, actively seek opportunities to show the love of Christ to others. Use the gifts and talents He has given you to bless others, and as you do this, you will experience the pure joy of Christ living out His life within you. Christ living through you will leave you bearing the fruit of the spirit, not just seasonally, but all year.

With God as our Director, let us wait well, my friend!

Meet Patricia Salmon

P atricia is a social butterfly. She loves God and loves people. She loves to share the Word of God with others telling them how an encounter with Jesus will change their lives for the better forever. She is in her true element when she is serving others. She enjoys cooking and volunteers her time doing so for the local soup kitchen at her church.

Patricia is a part-time real estate agent serving in New York, a full-time accountant, an international speaker, the author of her book "Woman Straightened Up" and co-author of "Waiting in the Pit I." She is a content creator who streams her content on her YouTube channel, "Woman Straightened Up."

For prayer or speaking engagements, you can reach out to me at *womanstraightenedup@gmail.com*.
Website www.womanstraightenedup.org

*"I wait for the LORD, my soul doth wait, and in his word do I hope." **(Psalms 130:5)***

Meet the Visionary

Hilette Virgo is a brand plucked from the fire. God has blessed her with the gift of writing, editing, organizing, networking, and connecting people.

She is a Christian life coach, international preacher, transformational speaker, three-times bestselling author, and the COO and editor-in-chief of GreatNest Publications. She is also the CEO of Hilette Virgo Motivates, a company that offers motivational services such as one-on-one coaching, group seminars, discovery sessions, leadership training, and keynotes.

Meet the Visionary

Hilette is on a mission to uplift, inspire and empower people to "Tap into their GEATNEST and soar into their GREATNESS" through her calling of writing, speaking, and coaching.

She believes that every soul that graced this earth possesses a wealth of inexhaustible potential waiting to be harnessed.

Known to her clients as "Mommy Eagle" and the "Book Doula," she is determined to convince everyone meets of their inner GREATNESS one written and spoken word at a time.

Her inspirationals: *Activating Her Eagle Instincts* and *Evoking Your Divine Dove* have blessed many hearts internationally. God trusted her with the three-part series, *Waiting in the Pit*.

As a faith-based publisher, editor, and ghostwriter, Hilette is committed to helping Christians globally to birth their memoirs, devotionals, poetry anthology, and other faith-based and inspirational books.

She can be contacted at:

- www.hilettevirgo.com
- Hilettevirgomotivates@gmail.com
- greatnestpublications@gmail.com

Made in the USA
Columbia, SC
27 July 2024